DATE DUE

WHEN WORDS HAVE LOST THEIR MEANING

WHEN WORDS HAVE LOST THEIR MEANING

Alzheimer's Patients Communicate through Art

RUTH ABRAHAM

Westport, Connecticut
London

Library of Congress Cataloging-in-Publication Data

Abraham, Ruth, 1943–
  When words have lost their meaning : Alzheimer's patients communicate through art /
Ruth Abraham.
    p.   cm.
  Includes bibliographical references and index.
  ISBN 0–275–97989–X (alk. paper)
  1. Alzheimer's disease.   2. Art therapy.   I. Title.
  RC523.A265   2005
  616.8'31065156—dc22   2004053438

British Library Cataloguing in Publication Data is available.

Library of Congress Catalog Card Number: 2004053438
ISBN: 0–275–97989–X

First published in 2005

Praeger Publishers, 88 Post Road West, Westport, CT 06881
An imprint of Greenwood Publishing Group, Inc.
www.praeger.com

Printed in the United States of America

For my husband, Ze'ev, and my three children, Jeffrey, Paula, and Danny.
You make life worthwhile.

CONTENTS

ILLUSTRATIONS

FIGURES

Chapter 1: Getting to Know the Alzheimer's Patient

Chapter 2: Does Art Therapy Really Help?

Chapter 3: The Therapeutic Hour: A Practical Guide

Chapter 5: Portraits: Three Case Studies

Tanya: Daring to Give and Take

Adam: Peek-a-Boo with Demons

Simon: Coming Out from Under the Covers

Chapter 7: A Personal Story

ACKNOWLEDGMENTS

I want to acknowledge my parents, who continue to live inside me, battling each other as always, though thankfully with less intensity as I grow older. My mother's sweetness and exceptional compassion and my father's maverick disregard for social consensus are their unwitting gifts that I carry with me and use as best I can.

The motto of my first therapist, Becky Davis, was "You never know," which proved to be true. I certainly never knew, during those early years of therapy, years of confusion and pain, that I would one day write a book. I wish she were alive to see it. Her parting has left a hole in my life.

I am grateful to the people who helped me during the process of research and writing. Professor Yoseph Hes gave me the opportunity to work in his department and kindly read the completed manuscript. Ruti Zuk was administrative head of the psychogeriatric center and had sufficient faith in me to permit me to work with patients in my own way. Tsippi Vainer Benaiah, Debbie Lahav, Chani Biran, and Rebecca Bergman generously read chapters and provided feedback. My husband tirelessly assisted and supported me during this long process—reading, typing, cutting, printing, and editing. It would have been a far less pleasant experience without his encouragement and loving support. I am so grateful. And, finally, the professionalism, enthusiasm, and gentle advice of my agent, Robbie Hare, made this work possible. One has to be lucky in life to meet someone who really believes in one, who supports and encourages one to transform dreams into realities. Such people have the power to change lives. There are few words to express the impact of such generosity. *Thank you* will have to suffice.

CLARIFICATION

The terms *Alzheimer's* and *dementia* have at times been used interchangeably in the text. *Dementia* is the more general term for decline from a previous intellectual level that interferes with a person's cognitive, emotional, and behavioral functioning. In itself it is not a disease but rather a group of symptoms related to a variety of physical conditions, such as multi-infarcts (strokes), brain tumors, Parkinson's disease, vitamin deficiency, and Alzheimer's. The great majority, though not all, of the patients with whom I worked over the years, suffered from dementia of the Alzheimer's type. Though dementias vary in regard to issues such as the cause of onset and speed of deterioration, ultimately the major symptoms—memory confusion, disruptions in verbal ability, disorganization—are present in all people afflicted with dementia.

The issue of gender is always problematic, and I have chosen to alternate between use of the male and female form. Though there are more women in most facilities (both patients and therapists), there is no reason to exclude the many men who were my patients or some of the male therapists who were my colleagues.

I have used the term *loved ones* a few times in the book, but I worry about the sentimentality of such terminology. Unfortunately, not everyone who is stricken with Alzheimer's is, literally, a loved one. Many spouses, siblings, and children who have had a lifetime of complex and painful familial relationships now find themselves in the role of unwilling, resentful caretaker as they still carry the baggage of unresolved past relationships with them.

I have sometimes used the word *patient* and sometimes *artist/patient*, largely in order to avoid repetitiveness. The problem with the term *patient* is that it harks back to the medical model, but most other options bother me equally. The by-now-accepted term *client* evokes the notion of a commodity to be sold and bought, which to me does not cover the interactions involved in art therapy. If it were not so clumsy, I would talk of a fellow traveler or of a person in need. *Artist/patient* acknowledges the fact that the person is in need and at the same time places value on the creative act.

In order to protect the identity of my patients, I have changed their names and removed their signatures from the artwork. Nonetheless, I think each one of them would have been terribly proud to know that their pictures were sufficiently important to have appeared in a book.

INTRODUCTION

Words strain
Crack and sometimes break
Under the burden under the tension.
—*T. S. Eliot*

Unfortunately, medical science has not yet provided any effective long-term treatment for Alzheimer's disease. In the absence of a much-hoped-for miracle drug, it is our responsibility to find ways to enhance the lives of those stricken with the illness. Current major therapeutic approaches consist of practical and emotional support and of strategies that help strengthen remaining capacities. Art therapy, a relatively new resource, sets out to do exactly these things, offering an additional means to bolster the humanity of the Alzheimer's patient. Art therapy proves to be a powerful medium because it bypasses the dominant verbal aspects of brain function. The work is based on the assumption that in spite of deterioration and advancing limitations, the dementia patient is nevertheless a person with an interior subjective world. The afflicted person, overwhelmed by an inability to articulate, can give voice to this inner world through the use of art materials. In providing that person with the symbolic language of art, an alternative channel for communication is opened. This is a vital gift when words have lost their meaning.

Art therapists working with dementia sufferers are just at the beginning of a struggle for acknowledgment and legitimacy as they introduce their skills into new territories. Hopefully, this book will bring art therapy into the care system, provide a channel through which therapists can increase their communication with patients, and bring new information and a measure of understanding to caregivers and loved ones who are increasingly cut off from Alzheimer's sufferers because of the dementia.

Art therapists maintain a fundamental belief in creativity as a defining principle of human life and aim to facilitate meaningful creative experiences rather than to produce "good" paintings. We talk of the importance of the *process* as opposed to the *product*. To elicit a personal mark, to become a catalyst for these creative assertions in individuals damaged by dementia, and to mine these residues of vitality and emotionality, is the basic mission of the dedicated art therapist. They nurse no illusions that the therapy can result in lasting changes in the personality structure, that patients can benefit from new insights, or that they can promote new coping strategies to deal with objective difficulties. Instead what art therapists do pursue is that which still exists, which has not yet been contaminated, and through encouraging personal expression, support the patient at his own particular level of functioning.

Through the period during which I worked as an art therapist in a psychogeriatric center, I must have unknowingly been nursing the idea of writing about the experience sometime in the future. Gathering my patients' artwork with no conscious plans of what to do with it, and unable to discard even seemingly trivial scribbles or messy pages of murky paint, I haphazardly stored them away. It is difficult to throw away productions that seem to emanate from real creative desire even if the pages themselves looked primitive or stereotypical. This reluctance to dispose of artwork has been influenced by years of working with different populations and witnessing the way in which pictures or sculptures become imbued with magical powers for the creator. The way even the most seemingly insignificant artwork is treasured was brought home to me by the child who requested the sculpture of "my father," years after she had squashed a piece of clay, seemingly casually, between her fingers. Choosing from a box of unlabeled remains of clay work, she was quite specific about which lump of clay was "the father." Equally, a simple pencil drawing on a small page can evoke emotions long after its creation, proving that it represented internal experiences meaningful to the creator at the time of its making. Alzheimer's patients, deprived of their memory, cannot sustain their connection to their art, but I can, and I did, and I simply could not discard the pages of work. What a treasure this collection turned out to be when I did finally decide that I wanted to share my experience, the lessons I had learned from it, and what I could teach others about it.

I actually came to work with Alzheimer's patients in a quite fortuitous manner. As a teacher in a postgraduate art therapy program, I was in the process of investigating facilities that worked with a range of disorders, so that I could recommend these as work placements for my students after the completion of their studies. Reluctantly, I admit, I visited the psychogeriatric center, fundamentally quite doubtful about the contribution that art, as therapy, could make to people suffering from what I knew to be an irreversible degenerative disease. For this visit, I had to overcome an unexamined resistance to face the depressing reality of the aging process exacerbated by dementia. The abrupt switch from skepticism to enthusiasm took me quite by surprise. Instead of the overwhelming picture of gloom and hopelessness that I anticipated as I walked with trepidation through the locked doors of the unit, I encountered a palpable atmosphere of gentleness and kindness. These qualities cannot be measured, neither are they considered valid therapeutic tools; certainly they are not mentioned much in psychological literature. However, the dedication of the staff members was heartwarming, directed as it was toward the confused and troubled people who, I knew, could find little place for themselves in the hurried world outside the facility. The staff, whether the kitchen workers, the coordinators of activities, social workers, psychologists, or medical team, all conveyed tolerance and forgiveness for the slowness, repetitions, and constant complaints of the patients. Therapists made themselves available to attend to often incoherent communications, sometimes with a hand placed gently on a patient's shoulder. They listened, answered, and consoled, and I witnessed grateful and smiling patients, who appeared to feel safe and protected. Soon after, quite unexpectedly, I became the art therapist at the center, and I remained in that position for the next eight years.

These years of work gave me an understanding of what it must be like to face the cruel losses of dementia. As I learned about the disruptions in functioning, the gradual damage to capacities, I was more able to react with compassion to the frustration, depression, and apathy that patients expressed. And slowly I began to see a more hopeful aspect. I saw that even human beings with very diminished capacities could live lives of contentment and satisfaction; that though many mechanisms are failing, there remain abilities and faculties through which to take pleasure in life. Art therapy, I became convinced, was a resource that could provide a means of expression of emotions, a tool to bolster self-image, and an alternative language of symbols, metaphors, images, color, line, and form through which patients could communicate.

The last decade has seen an onslaught of information, both in scientific publications and the popular press, about the "new epidemic," the "ravages of dementia," and the "erosion that sweeps over the brain," as well as anxiety-provoking warnings that we are "racing against time." Statistical figures show us the growing danger that each of us might face this "long goodbye." Theories abound, none yet conclusively proven, about the cause of the spread of plaques and tangles that attack the synapses of the brain, interfering with transmission of messages from one neuron to the other. According to Madeleine Nash (2000) the disease has affected an estimated 20 million people around the world, and the number will triple by the year 2050 as the population ages (p. 52). And we continue to hope that we will not be among those who have to suffer this painfully drawn out, irreversible, and ultimately fatal condition that causes cognitive, emotional, and behavioral deterioration.

Elizabeth Cohen (2003), in her deeply touching memoir, *The House on Beartown Road*, warns:

> People aren't prepared for what is coming. It will hit them as it has me. An army of the forgetful is about to march on the whole country. . . . If it hasn't happened to you, then it must seem so abstract. The words *aging population* just don't have the urgent ring of *tornado, hurricane, famine,* or *flood.* But it is the same thing. Disaster is about to strike, hard and fast, and when it does it will leave us reeling and vulnerable as a society. It will cripple our medical system; it will absorb all sorts of resources. It will exhaust the whole nation. (p. 192)

This might smack of exaggeration, a strongly emotional response from a daughter witnessing, firsthand, the agonizing, slow loss of her father as she once knew him. But Alzheimer's disease is indeed an epidemic and one that society is ill-equipped to deal with. It is making huge demands on the allocation of funds as people are living longer, and savings that once promised a life of security are often consumed by expensive long-term care. The modern Western world has lost much of its sense of community, so that old people have little chance of enjoying the support of an extended clan or the consolation that might come from continued social participation. The dispersal of families is, in many cases, further disrupting the support system, leaving many people who have a relative ailing with Alzheimer's essentially alone to deal with the hardships. Societal attitudes are permeated by ageism, a blight not dissimilar to racism, in which the old are attributed a group of negative characteristic that disregard the personal traits of the individual, relegating him to one predefined negative category. Our society has failed to develop any rituals or discourse through which to process the reality and finality of decay and death, so the inevitable darker facets of life are experienced as dangerous territory to be avoided. It is easier to turn our backs on suffering and illness about which we can do little, for which there is no cure, in which deterioration is unavoidable. Contact with those who are elderly, weak, and vulnerable, brings up fears of our own future frailty and dependence. When we live in a world of pressures, ambitions, egocentrism, pleasure seeking, and work demands, the sudden reality of a parent, spouse, or sibling stricken with dementia is enormously challenging. And if to begin with we didn't care very much for this ailing family member, if this is the end stage of a long, negative relationship with residues of resentment and hurt, then the extra burden of the disease is a cause for more unpleasantness. If we did feel affection for them, if they have been loving, supporting, presences during our lives, the gradual change as they progress into a state of more dependency and helplessness, is shocking and sad, to say the least. And yet, we have to deal with the reality, if in the first case only out of obligation, or in the second, because of our love and commitment.

While I was honing my skills as an art therapist, learning how to initiate creativity with Alzheimer's patients, it was becoming clear that my elderly mother was herself in the process of cognitive decline due to the disease. I had to mine different abilities in order to deal with her illness on a more personal and emotional level. This firsthand experience added a different dimension to my growing familiarity with the process of the disease. In the years that followed her diagnosis, I tried to be a good-enough daughter to my ailing mother. It still hurts when I think of the times that I was harsh and unforgiving, when I could no longer bear the endless questions, when I slipped in to see her and left hastily after ten minutes, smarting from her pleading "so soon?" as she grabbed onto my arm. Many people are compelled to tell the story of this difficult relationship for their own healing purposes, seeking self-forgiveness or extracting personal meaning out of their encounter with Alzheimer's. Others, haunted by the years of physical and emotional distress, desire to use their painfully acquired knowledge to inform and console those who are in the midst of the one-way journey. Diana Friel McGowin, in *Living in the Labyrinth* (1993), wrote a rare account of her own struggle with the disease when she first became aware of her memory loss and bouts of disorientation. Linda Grant (1999), John Bayley (1999), Sue Miller (2003), Elizabeth Cohen (2003), and Eleanor Cooney (2003) all recount the havoc caused by the invasion of the illness on their beloved parents and spouses and the agonizing struggle to take care of them without allowing themselves to fall apart in the process. Other writers have woven these themes into their novels: Kate Jennings in *Moral Hazard* (2002), the Japanese author Sawako Ariyoshi in *The Twilight Years* (1972), and Michael Ignatieff in *Scar Tissue* (1994). The drive to record, to gather the pieces of one's experience and turn them into a coherent and consoling story is what gave birth to my own brief, personal contribution to the ever-growing library of accounts and memoirs. It was born out of a need for the proverbial closure after my mother's death, a way of joining the community of caretakers still reeling from the "enemy of forgetting" that, as Cohen says, "steals what a person truly owns; it takes the life he has lived, leaving him stranded on the island of the present" (p. 5). The story of my mother's illness quite naturally runs through my understanding and learning in the professional world, providing insights without the distancing and potential intellectual escape and barriers of the professional role. I wonder what sort of therapist I would have been had my mother not taught me all she did through those long years of her struggle with the illness. Ultimately, these quite different experiences, professional and personal, intellectual and emotional, are blended together in the book.

The story of Alzheimer's disease is one of increasing loss that finally damns the patient to complete helplessness after the breakdown of mental and bodily functions. As the patient is diminished by the illness, his experience of the world is altered, as are his behavior and his emotional response to it. Increasingly isolated by the inability to manipulate and understand language, often overwhelmed in any verbal question-and-answer situation, the patient can give voice, without threat, to his inner life through the use of art materials.

One of the earliest signs of Alzheimer's is a growing loss of short-term memory, a difficulty retaining and recalling recent information. However, there is more than one kind of memory, such as those of feelings, sensibilities, unverbalized moral codes, and intuitions. These are memories of a different kind, located and processed in the right hemisphere of the brain, where they remain intact for far longer than does memory in the verbal left brain. The onset of dementia, with its telltale signs of misplacing objects, difficulty in recalling names, uncomfortable inability to recall recent incidents, until the final, almost totally vegetative state is followed by a long process of deterioration. The official diagnosis is usually followed by a mostly static seven-year period during which the level of impairment is to a large extent maintained. During the subsequent years—fifteen or more—there is significant deterioration and severe cognitive decline. The initial seven-year period provides a window of opportunity, during which, though the patient may be confused and forgetful, he continues to have an accessible emotional world. Though their emotions may be less richly textured, patients continue to express desires, hurts, personal tastes, and views on life, as well as a capacity and interest in relating to those around them. Supportive therapies can sustain these existing abilities and protect the patient from the sort of neglect that would spiral him into much more profound dementia, compounded by isolation, loneliness, and depression.

MORAL DILEMMAS

This book is directed in part to the audience of professional art therapists, because it outlines and details the craft of art therapy when applied to the dementia population. It will also be of use to many of the other professional caregivers involved with Alzheimer's care, such as psychiatrists, psychologists, and occupational therapists, all of whom can benefit by discovering another way into the inner world of their patients. But I also hoped to imbue the book with moral and ethical questions that should be of concern to anyone involved with the aging process and the provisions made for the old, the frail, and the diminished. Because there is no way out of old age except through an untimely early death, each society has to articulate ways in which it copes with the last stage of life. The legendary Eskimo solution, in which those who do not function adequately are cast out from the community, strikes us with its heartless practicality. Fictions of the old being led away to a barren, cold place to die fill us with horror. Velma Wallis highlights this tragic dismissal of the aged in her book *Two Old Women: An Alaskan Legend of Betrayal, Courage, and Survival* (1993). In it, she retells the story of two elderly women abandoned by their tribe and the ensuing guilt and self-repugnance experienced by the tribe when they reunite with the women who survived because of their fierce determination. The tribe then has to face their moral failure and attempt to make reparations for their heartlessness. At the other extreme are the societies in which the aged continue to be respected, cared for, and loved by the younger members of the tribe. They are seen as sources of wisdom and even valued as essential bridges between life and death.

The attitude of the contemporary Western world lies somewhere between these two attitudes. Our sense of morality dictates that we take care of our aged, an ethical commitment instilled by the biblical commandment to "Honor thy father and thy mother," which must include taking responsibility for them in their final dependent and disabled condition. Yet, there are times when our solutions are reminiscent of the chilling notions of Eskimo society: millions of frail aged live on their own, often abandoned by family, and many are marginalized in protected facilities, removed from the rest of the community in an attenuated version of "being led away." Tom Kitwood in his book *Dementia Reconsidered* (1997) presents his case for better care for Alzheimer's patients. He rails against the "malignant social psychology" found in dementia care (p. 11) with the callous disregard for human dignity and integrity, and pleads for what he calls a culture of care. In this new culture he believes that we would not pathologize people who have dementia but focus instead on the uniqueness of each person with respect and compassion, acknowledging the essential social aspect of all existence, even a diminished one. In a similar manner, Oliver Sacks (1985) seeks the human, the personal, and the emotional in each patient stricken with bizarre symptoms and acute limitations. They too are beings with longings, desires, tastes, and loves, if only someone would see through the confusion to the human kernel and discover the shape of a person still experiencing life but unable to articulate who he is. Sacks contemplates the "undiminished possibility of reintegration by art, by communion, by touching the human spirit . . . and this can be preserved in what seems at first a hopeless state of neurological devastation" (p. 37).

As we face the gradual reversal of roles in which our once active, dependable, and vibrant parents now turn to us for decision making, advice, and support, we become increasingly aware that we are next in line. We fear that what we neglect now will come back to haunt us when we are old and dependent, that what we prepare now, what we invest in, in terms of resources and commitment, will come back to us when it is our time to seek assistance. When our strength has waned and our capacity to initiate has diminished, we will wish for others to honor us with concern and devotion. Yet very few of us will be fortunate enough to continue to live within the young, active world we have occupied for so long. We will be separated from the community, having to make a new life essentially with other old people.

This uncomfortable realization was highlighted for me when my mother became more helpless and dependent and Tessa entered our lives as a live-in caretaker. Tessa had left her children with her extended family in the Philippines, sacrificing her relationship with them for many years, in order to increase her income and provide them with a better education. She took on a strange, complex place in my mother's life as well as in mine, entering into a deeply committed partnership with me, a mix of sister and friend, when I felt so alone with my mother's illness. She cared for my mother with devotion and love. It was she who smiled with me, sharing my pride when my mother managed to remember a song from the past, she who had tears in her eyes when my mother lay groaning in pain and could not explain what hurt. I felt both deep compassion for Tessa, who had made these familial sacrifices for economic reasons, as well as guilt that I, instead of her children, should benefit from her nurturing. Imagine my surprise when she confided apologetically one day that she felt sorry for me. She was concerned, she said, that no one would be there to look after me when I became old and helpless like my mother, whereas she would have her entire village around her to take care of her. What a twist! In spite of my privileged life, she pitied me. Tessa didn't know of anyone in her community who had had Alzheimer's, but then she admitted she wouldn't have noticed if they had. No one has any intellectual expectation of the old, nor is there a demand on them to be enlightened about current events or to carry on a conversation. They sit on the balcony and talk with contemporaries, rock the babies, and watch the young people as they go about their business. They continue to live within the community of the young, no longer taking an active part in the daily grind of life, but neither discarded nor neglected.

THE IMPORTANCE OF THE IMAGE

When a disability limits the use of language, images become particularly significant both as a means to communicate emotional material and as a means to heal. Ancient shamans used the imagination as a powerful source of healing, and today it is widely accepted that the mind plays a major part in influencing healthy functioning. Jeanne Achterberg (1985) writes about the growing medical and psychological consensus regarding the negative power of the imagination on well-being; agreement that fear, anxiety, and depression increase the likelihood of ill health, and that there is a causal relationship between negative states of mind and the diminished resistance to disease. It seems reasonable to assume that the reverse is also true. There is a renewed "focus on the imagination as . . . a potent aspect of healing," says Achterberg (1985, p. 4), the imagination having a pronounced effect on the body, yielding "power over life and death" (p. 3). Using the latest data from modern medicine, she shows that what has often been considered "worthless" medical intervention—suggestion, placebo drugs, and imagery—is responsible for major changes in biochemistry. For instance, mental rehearsal of an event, or an experience, can evoke major muscular changes, increase blood pressure, and cause changes in brain waves. Phyllis J. Jarvinen and Steven R. Gold (1979) found that it was possible to reduce levels of depression by encouraging severely depressed patients to attend to nondepressive daydreams. Thought, ideas, fantasies, and images seem to have a more concrete physical impact than any skeptic would believe.

The right hemisphere of the brain makes use of images and symbolic language to process material and remains intact far longer than the verbal left brain, once Alzheimer's sets in. Through the image, the aphasic patient (one whose language ability is to varying degrees compromised) can be provided with experiences that favorably influence his well-being and self-image in spite of his being unable to verbalize such positive feelings. This supports the case for the benefit of the use of images in art activities, particularly for Alzheimer's victims who are in the process of losing their verbal capacities.

THE IMPORTANCE OF THE ARTWORK

Throughout this book, I have included examples of the artwork of my artist/patients in order to demonstrate the therapy in process and to display the surprising beauty of the creative act where one might least expect it. Often, against all odds, and in spite of eyesight severely damaged by cataracts or glaucoma, hands that shake from Parkinson's, pains of arthritis, or general weakness, a small but wondrous work will be born. A sigh of satisfaction will emerge as patients gaze in surprise at their success. And though moments later they might already have forgotten that they are the creators of this work, the experience has been had. We take it on faith that the memory of that experience exists at some experiential level beyond the moment, yet it is not only faith that we rely on. We see the very gradual acquisition of minor skills and familiarity with the materials over a period of time, indicating that there is an accumulation of memories. As some patients gravitate independently toward the art room, one might ask them why they are there and receive a puzzled shrug of the shoulders. Yet, moments later, without direction from the therapist, a few will have returned to their usual seat, will pull a page toward themselves, choose a color, and begin smearing enthusiastically—something that would have been unexpected a few months earlier. This is a sort of remembering, though one most of them cannot articulate.

The central documentation of the therapy process must be the artwork itself and the stories it tells. Without these one cannot claim respect for the images or argue for their value as tools for therapy. Describing a picture and the details of its contents never has the impact of the actual artwork, or at least a photographic documentation of it. But on their own, the pictures also lack the power to convince. The combination of the artwork, the circumstances of its birth, some understanding of the world of the creator, and the context of its creation, all tell a greater story than a glance at an image on a page can reveal.

A story will illustrate this point. Very recently, I visited a psychogeriatric unit to observe the work of a member of the staff who is in charge of art activities. Shelly is not an art therapist but an inspiring art teacher who has a deeply optimistic belief in her patients' capacities. She has an enthusiastic and intuitive ability that facilitates exceptionally lively creative activity. Her room is a buzz of activity and color, and the dynamic Shelly responds to requests, advising, energizing, and encouraging. As I stood admiring some of the works, a handsome, robust man in his early seventies strolled into the room and greeted Shelly with a friendly, collegial smile. I recognized him immediately as a familiar flamboyant artist and popular raconteur. I presumed he was there to contribute his artistic assistance to the unit, stretched out my hand, received a warm handshake, and reminded him of our various mutual friends and past meetings. Though his answer was friendly and gallant, I quickly picked up a revealing flatness in his polite words that I recognized as confabulation, a way of using language to hide the confusion and lack of comprehension that people with dementia experience. My heart sank when I realized that Paul was not a volunteer to the unit but a very confused dementia patient. Remembering various events at which the charming, often provocative, and entertaining artist had been the center of attention, and observing him now, still so physically youthful, was chilling. "I'd better go now. They're coming. You know. Them." he said to Shelly with a tense smile. On the table lay a beautifully drawn picture with richly shaded forms and well-articulated images, the pencil work of a skilled artist. "I did this yesterday," he said, "but I'm still working on it." It was a landscape, a hill covered with trees and leafy growth. On top of the hill stood a proud goat, formed with the casual graphic skill acquired by artists through years of experience. I was delighted to see such abilities still intact and chose to relate particularly to the wonderfully crafted goat. Paul looked exasperated, discarding my admiration, and pointed out a tiny, primitive figure at the bottom of the hill, embedded somewhat in an indentation. "It's him," he said. "He doesn't know where to go. Look. He's lost. His feet are in the water. He's the one," he insisted. What I heard was the urgent desire to share his concern for the lost man, to show something that was significant to him within the picture rather than to impress the viewer with his skills. I learned that he had actually drawn this picture months before and had resolutely refused to create any artwork since, instead staring daily at the lost man, asking, "Which way should he go?" Paul, it appeared, had a far greater hunger than showing off his abilities. What he needed was to express what he felt as he mourned his artistic losses. In a sense, and quite unconsciously, he was begging to turn the observer's gaze away from the past, from what he knew no longer exists. He needed one's gaze to focus on the poorly articulated, childishly drawn little man, threatened by the waters of the river. Paul was not my patient, and I was only a casual visitor, but I did respond to his plea by turning my attention to the lost man, thus acknowledging Paul's current feelings of diminishment.

This incident illustrates the complexity of the different meanings that a page of artwork can acquire, the importance of the context in which the work was done, and the different responses that it elicits, depending on the agenda of the facilitator. Artwork can have therapeutic value of very differing kinds for very different reasons. Sometimes the artist/patient might need confirmation of his skill and creative ability, to be encouraged and admired. Another may need to communicate, with no less urgency, his sense of failure, and disappointment. One patient will want to share his pride and pleasure; another, his despair and pain. In the former, the gaze of admiration will complete the creative act. In the latter, the gaze moves toward the patient's suffering and loneliness, and the gift is in the form of an encounter in which the "other" does not shift his eyes away from the suffering but, through compassion and acceptance, provides a container for the emotions. Paul's world was fragmenting, and his truth was no longer the well-structured goat, but that of disorganization and disorientation. It is very tempting to admire, to be smitten by the creativity and talent of one's patients. For Paul, such admiration only increased his loneliness and sense of invisibility.

We see in this vignette a significant difference between the art teacher and the art therapist. Shelly's agenda was improving the skills and the artistic productions of the patient, thus providing hours of pleasure as well as confirmation for them regarding their capacities. The art therapist has a different agenda. While the beautifully crafted picture is always a pleasure, it is not the main issue; encounter is. The understanding of the patient's emotional process will profoundly influence one's understanding of it and one's response to it, and it is this that transforms the art activity into a form of therapy.

A PLACE FOR OPTIMISM

Finally, my intention has been to introduce a thread of optimism into this book. The harsh diagnosis of Alzheimer's does not imply that all is lost. From the moment of diagnosis until profound deterioration sets in, that point at which meaningful communication is almost impossible, there is much opportunity to alleviate suffering and enrich lives that otherwise would be discarded as useless. Artistic skill is often surprisingly preserved, even after damage to the brain. Professional artists suffering from varying types of brain damage may still produce work of high quality, though the style and standard of the productions may have altered. Willem de Kooning, the great abstract expressionist painter of the twentieth century, continued to paint long after Alzheimer's had set in. Some of these paintings began to look "weary and thin," but many were still "deft" and "gorgeous," sparkling in the exhibition halls, in spite of the artist's increasing dislocation from the world (Plagens, 1997, p. 54) For amateur artists, though similar changes of style are seen, the artistic ability often persists in spite of impairment to certain cognitive skills. There are rare cases, such as in frontotemporal dementia, in which a period of exceptional creativity accompanies the onset of dementia, even as the patients begin to lose their ability to use language. Apparently, damage to one part of the brain may lead to enhanced functioning in another. Bruce L. Miller and Margaret Mary Clausen (1998) point out, "We never think about the strengths of patients. We only think of the weaknesses. Now I always ask if there is anything patients are doing very well, or better than before" (p. 3).

When one enters a geriatric unit for dementia patients, one will be witness to diverse scenes. An old man with a strong Parkinsonian tremor sits close to the locked exit door, staring outside longingly, with dull and lonely eyes. A tiny woman stands at the main desk, barely able to see over the top of it, pleading with the secretary that she wants to go home, demanding that she phone her mother to come and get her. A robust-looking, slim man paces backward and forward, mumbling aggressively, while two women, pushing their walkers, argue nastily, gesticulating with bony fingers, stammering their indignation, each determined to get through the door before the other. But in this very same space, there are other scenes to be viewed. Three women sit involved in a conversation, maybe complaining about the food, or the staff, but making contact nevertheless. An old man has taken a frail woman by the arm and is leading her into a room for the "current affairs" group meeting. At the door of the art room, a woman consults with the art teacher about the appropriate place to hang her drawings. You can cast your eye this way or that. The choice is yours, and ultimately it will affect the way you feel about the contribution of such a facility and the value you place on the care of Alzheimer's patients.

On one occasion, a long-time member of my art group informed me that she was bringing along a friend to join our sessions. I had little choice but to agree, since this practically aphasic woman already had her new friend by the hand; the man was a newcomer to the unit with whom she had instantly bonded and for whom she began to jealously guard a seat next to hers whenever she came to future meetings. This woman and man were both severely confused and dislocated, and yet they had formed a bond, and though I doubt they ever learned each other's names, they had embarked on a new relationship. They had a life and were still capable of new loyalties and affection. These are the healthy, lively aspects of functioning that often evade the attention of caretakers whose attention is taken up with the illness and pathology.

While working on this book I was, inadvertently, assisted by simple but challenging questions that people repeatedly posed and that forced me to re-examine and articulate important issues. One that I heard often was, "Does it really help?" and similarly, "Is it really worth it?" But who is to tell us when a life is no longer worth living? It is only if one drops such judgments and sustains the belief that there is life to be had in spite of limitations that one can work with people who find themselves in such a diminished position. Ultimately we are all decaying and dying, and the question is what we do while we wait for that to happen. The medical world faces similar dilemmas as it seeks to improve its palliative care for the terminally ill. Physicians find it hard to provide care for patients they can't cure, though easing the end of life is surely no less important to a good doctor. While we might wait optimistically for a cure, we have a chance to enhance people's lives and say, "Yes, art therapy helps!" and, "Yes, it is a worthwhile endeavor!" So though this book concerns the harrowing predicament of Alzheimer's, it is ultimately a book about life, color, and creativity and of art therapy as a means of providing a forum for their flowering.

1

※

GETTING TO KNOW
THE ALZHEIMER'S PATIENT

People diagnosed with Alzheimer's disease are largely talked of as lost selves, ghosts, absences, and masks. This global description does no justice to the various stages of the disease, the unequal progression of the deterioration, and the manner in which different personality types respond to the gradual degeneration of their minds. Descriptions that disregard the personal aspect of the illness reduce the multitude of patients to one category, depriving them of their individuality. The art therapist will be exposed to many individuals who will challenge this global preconception of the inaccessible, blank-eyed Alzheimer's sufferer. It is through accounts of personal experience with a dementia sufferer, in fiction and in memoirs, or in detailed case histories, that we get a picture not of an illness but of social beings struggling with the invasion of illness. Improved diagnostic testing makes it easier to detect the onset of dementia at an earlier stage, so the patient that the therapist encounters might actually be aware of the commencement of the disease. Carefully attired and attentive to his surroundings, he will probably be anxious and ashamed of already subtly diminishing functioning. But if he is made to feel safe, he might be keen to express his difficulties with a compassionate listener. On the other hand, there are patients who drag themselves listlessly into the art room, staring frozenly ahead, barely responding to their surroundings. Some patients are sociable and communicative, struggling sometimes to make sense of their thoughts, yet openly expressing affection and interest, while others will criticize, accuse, and argue viciously over the disputed ownership of a crayon. We must not forget that the troubled person in our midst has a history, past relationships, a profession, and articulated attitudes. At one time, he earned money, brought up children, had loves, and experienced disappointments. Although he might not be able to share his biography with us, he can, through art, share another sort of information, another way of telling about himself. Visual art will reflect its maker; preferences in composition, choice of color, attraction to specific materials, and rhythm of lines are all ways of sharing perceptions and inner life. Each aspect of graphic style communicates a parallel aspect of one's internal world, and images are a declaration of desires, fantasies, and dreams. Through art, the patient has an opportunity to declare that somewhere within his fractured world there reside qualities embedded in his core personality structure.

While taking care to relate to a person rather than an illness, to a personality rather than a symptom, the therapist must at the same time have a clear picture of the general progressive course of Alzheimer's disease and its anticipated stages of deterioration, in order to place the patient within a medical context. Thus the therapist must avail herself of two maps for guidance: the character of the particular patient, which is the product of a lifetime of experiences, and knowledge about the stages of Alzheimer's disease and how it affects the workings of the mind, including thinking, emotion, and behavior. A disease, says Oliver Sacks (1985), "is never a mere loss or excess—there is always a reaction, on the part of the affected organism or individual, to restore, to replace, to compensate for and to preserve its identity" (p. 4). Ultimately there is always interplay between the disease and the person who is responding to it. Were it not so, the therapist would have a neutral and equal reaction to all patients, all arousing the same emotional response. The fact is, that despite the many common features and behavior of all Alzheimer's patients, the forgetting and the accusations and the repeated questions, therapists have widely different feelings for each of them, from extreme fondness and affection for some to antagonism and hostility toward others. Clearly, the deterioration does not entirely eliminate core personal characteristics. This personality, this voice, this existence is what one hopes to vitalize during the therapy, whether it is the pleasing personality of a loving and generous man or the less pleasant, aggressive, or passive personality of another.

In the early days of my work, an incident occurred that would be repeated with some variations over the years; it is one that highlights the distinction that needs to be made between the personal and the medical aspects of the people we work with. Lisa, an extremely cultured and very gentle elderly European lady, thrived in the art room. She constantly expressed gratitude for the opportunity given her to play, to be creative, and to find meaning through the rich explorations of art. She always struggled with the limitations imposed on her by the disease and managed to produce some delicate, whimsical drawings of which she was immensely proud and that were such a reflection of her personality. We have a large, round wastepaper bin in the confined space of the art room, and during one of the sessions, this educated and refined woman stood up, and before I could grasp what she was about to do, she had hitched up her skirt, taken down her panties and was urinating in the basket, whose shape she had associated with a toilet bowl. A previous version of herself, before the onslaught of Alzheimer's, no doubt would have been horrified by such behavior. Her action was not connected with personal issues, the dynamics of the therapy, aggression, or unconscious communication. It was an act that could be attributed totally to the disease that had damaged her perception and judgment. Exposing her to the inappropriateness of her act would have shamed her for no good reason. Knowing this helped me to ignore the bizarre behavior as best I could, quietly remove the basket from the room, and continue to relate to the undamaged parts of this sensitive and creative lady.

Alzheimer's disease is not a static condition; it runs a course of devastation that spans years. The symptoms don't appear in a totally predictable manner but rather affect each individual in differing patterns and at different rates. In the early stage (two–three years' duration), the patient might retain a well-functioning outward appearance that masks the illness from the onlooker, so that the dementia is usually only diagnosed in retrospect, when families of patients report what, in time, is seen as strange, atypical behavior that had previously been overlooked. There may be difficulties remembering names, faces, events, and words, confusion with telling time, significant decline in everyday functioning, and emotional changes such as depression and increased passivity, all of which are changes typically mentioned by referring families. The downside of improved diagnostic testing and early detection of Alzheimer's is that patients' greater insight inevitably arouses sadness, panic, anger, and fear as they understand what lies ahead of them. In the middle stage of approximately seven years' duration, patients can still be cared for at home but may attend day clinics where they can socialize and take part in various activities that boost their self esteem, preserve a sense of pride and dignity as productive adults, and provide a means of communication that somewhat alleviates the overwhelming sense of isolation that the condition brings with it. During this extended period, the patient may be confused and forgetful but continue to have an accessible and communicable emotional world provided that he is given a compassionate and supportive environment. In the final stage (which can last up to fifteen years), the deterioration so diminishes capacities that institutionalization is usually required and the last months and weeks are often spent in a helpless, vegetative state. It is during the middle period that art therapy can most enrich the quality of many lives.

In order to facilitate maximum creative pleasure and more sensitively guide the patient to particular materials and particular exercises, it is important for the therapist to assess the patients abilities at any point in the illness. The internal world of a person stricken with Alzheimer's changes constantly. He cannot rely, with the confidence of the healthy, on his memory, his perceptions, and his judgment. Such basic changes must be kept in mind in order to adapt oneself to often bizarre and sometimes insulting behavior. I have witnessed even experienced staff in the dementia-care facility, reacting with outrage when a patient accused them of having stolen their possessions. Restating the problem of the patient's altered perceptions and poor judgment helps to replace the indignation of having been falsely accused with understanding and compassion. I once removed all my rings before beginning a session working with clay, only to discover after the session was over that they had all been taken. How could I be angry with the gentleman who had stuffed the shiny objects into his pocket, telling us that these belonged to his wife and he was returning them to her? If one had a deeper understanding of the peculiar logic of his failing cognitive functions, one could only empathize with his distress when the items were taken away.

Though loss of memory is the first and most familiar symptom of the Alzheimer's patient, there is an array of other invasions that gradually destroy normal functioning.

MEMORY LOSS

The early disruptive and unnerving memory loss of Alzheimer's becomes devastating in its later and more severe forms. It affects registration, comprehension, storage of any new information, retention over a period of time, and retrieval. Because of the complex nature of memory and its delicate operation, any casual appraisals of the malfunctioning could be inaccurate. A person who doesn't remember what has just recently been said might actually have an impaired ability to concentrate, which interfered with his ability to focus on the piece of communicated information. On the other hand, he might not have understood what was said to him in the first place, or alternately he might have heard, understood, and remembered but have problems with retrieval of information. It is very important to constantly try and distinguish which of these difficulties is hampering his functioning, so as to guide him appropriately in the art activities. If his short-term memory is profoundly damaged, there is no alternative other than to constantly repeat and remind. If experience shows us that the patient has a problem with comprehension, we need to repeat explanations, possibly changing our words, simplifying the sentences, approaching the information input differently, by demonstration or by giving concrete examples, rather than just using more words.

When we talk of memory loss, we need to ask what sort of memory is retained and how it can be accessed and utilized. It is important to keep in mind, as various capacities are lost, that there are parts of the brain that continue to function, though they cannot be accessed through verbal channels. A simple but innovative experiment by the American psychiatrist Louis Tinnin (1990) illustrates how information, emotion, and memories stored in one hemisphere of the brain, might remain inaccessible to the other hemisphere. A simple learning task was given to subjects while their left hemisphere was anesthetized. When the anesthesia wore off, they were incapable of using language to communicate the material that was learned, though they could retrieve this through right-hemisphere activity such as visual recognition of pictures or touching certain objects. This indicates that one can know and feel and experience and even remember certain content, yet be unable to communicate it verbally. Because the brain does not operate as a uniform whole the right and left hemispheres may each have memories of which the other side is unaware. When working with Alzheimer's patients, one is trying to access memories and feeling states about which the rational, verbal left brain might not know. Tom Kitwood (1997) says that "memory may have faded, but something of the past is known; identity remains intact, because others hold it in place; thoughts may have disappeared, but there are still interpersonal processes; feelings are expressed and meet a validating response."

LANGUAGE DISRUPTION

The harshest consequence of the earlier disruption of left-brain functioning is the gradual loss of the effective ability to communicate verbally, which damns the sufferer to a world of increasing isolation. Most social interaction, which essentially depends on effective manipulation of language in order to communicate, becomes scrambled. The subjective experience (which one can only assume through empathic listening) is that of being lost somewhere within oneself, with no possibility of being found. The Alzheimer's patient will begin a sentence in an attempt to explain his anger or grief, but as he progresses one sees his words failing him, leading him further and further into a maze of confusion, helplessness, and frustration. Whoever is trying to make sense of this communication might find himself drawn into his own confusion as he attempts to understand and make sense of the fractured words, and gradually he too may give up in frustration. The art therapist relinquishes some of the attempt to communicate through explanations and logical understanding. He concentrates instead on the skills, powers, and intelligence of the right brain, where nonverbal images, rather than words, are used to process information. The right brain was traditionally referred to as the minor hemisphere, assumed to be less involved in human functioning than the supposedly superior rational, linear processes of the verbal left brain. In fact there is much to indicate that "survival, as well as rehabilitation, is significantly more likely following damage to the left hemisphere than to the right, indicating that life is more dependent upon the functions of the right brain" (Achterberg, 1985, p. 122). Art therapy reclaims the importance of right-brain functioning which, in Alzheimer's, remains vital long after the harshest disruptions of Alzheimer's.

Difficulties with verbal communication are pervasive and come in different forms, beginning with simple muddling of sentences all the way to total *aphasia*, in which there is complete loss of the use or understanding of language. A wide range of other difficulties can be experienced, among them the common problem of *anomia*, in which the patient cannot find an appropriate word, even though he knows what he wants to say, and *paraphasia*, which is the problem of interchanging words that sound alike (nurse interchanged with purse) or words that fall into the same category (wife instead of mother). Patients routinely resort to *confabulation*, a nonsensical invention, when they are trying to cover their inability to develop a logical sentence. Because none of these reflects an emotional problem but all are a response to disrupted mental functioning, it is of no help to try and correct these illogicalities. Doing so only causes further embarrassment to the patient who is trying so hard to retain his dignity.

PERCEPTUAL DISTORTION

The disease gradually damages perception, the very basic capacity necessary to interpret or make meaning out of the sensory information entering the brain. It can result in the inability to recognize even familiar objects. Eventually, parts of the patient's own body can be experienced as alien objects that have no meaning. The damage and distortion in perception obviously affects memory, since one has to perceive accurately in order to retain information. It can be observed behaviorally in confusions that occur during art sessions, when patients try to drink the paint or put oil pastels in their mouths, confusing them with beverages or food. Certain patients cannot perceive the edge of the page as a boundary; they may draw on a neighbor's page or even on another person's body, no longer perceiving the difference between the self and the other. The decline in perceptual capacity is expressed graphically in the artwork in many ways.

Simplification

In simplification, images are reduced to their simplest, most basic elements, without any elaboration. These images are often infantile, showing a

Figure 1.1. Simplification. Eyes, ears, and a nose are represented in basic form, with no perceptible expression. The flower consists of a simple circle of petal shapes.

discrepancy between the drawing and what would be expected even in an artistically inexperienced person of this age (Figure 1.1).

Fragmentation

In fragmentation, images are constructed of parts that do not connect and that are often floating in different parts of the page. Often the work begins with a clear image but slowly disintegrates into confusion (Figure 1.2).

Distortion

Distorted images are characterized by inconsistencies, illogicalities, and confusion. Though some parts of a face or torso may be well represented, there will often appear, inexplicably, a grotesque element that seems to have no

Figure 1.2. Fragmentation. Lines that begin as the hair on the head float away and become part of the background.

connection to the original image. While in some cases a feature of the face is excluded, in others it may be either magnified or diminished, with complete loss of proportion (Figure 1.3).

Perseveration

Perseveration, in which art activities takes the form of repetition of lines or elements, indicates an inability to end an activity once begun. Short memory span might cause the patient to lose track of his intentions, so that he continues without a conception of when to stop. Oftentimes, a portrait or landscape will be well articulated, but a patient who does not know when to stop will draw lines or introduce color that will slowly contaminate the initial image. Another tendency is to draw one image and then repeat it a few

Figure 1.3. Distortion. The top part of the face, including the eyes and nose, is fairly well articulated, whereas the mouth is huge and exceeds the contour lines of the face, resulting in a bizarre, grotesque image.

times on the same page. A Holocaust survivor who had lost his entire family and community in World War II drew a repetitive series of heads (Figure 1.4). It was difficult to know how much of the repetition was due to the fairly common phenomenon of perseverative behavior and how much was the expression of his personal theme of multiple losses.

The therapist in such situations will face a dilemma. Should one stop the patient before he begins to "destroy" a well-articulated image and thus save the "successful" art product? Or does one resist intervening and respect the patient's need to continue working even at the risk of a disappointing result? There are no formulaic solutions to this, and the decision will depend on the particular patient and one's assessment of his needs. One should obviously intervene before excessive frustration leads to passive resignation, and it is up to the therapist to decide when intervention is an imposition and when it is the very help the patient needs in order to regain control.

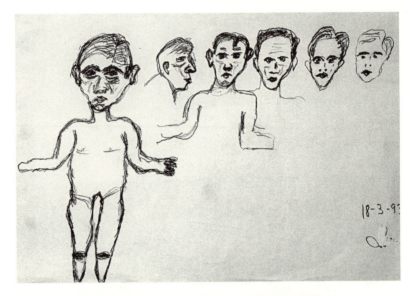

Figure 1.4. Perseveration. The patient succeeds in drawing a full figure but then continues drawing a row of heads, one next to the other.

Boundary Confusion

Faulty perception results in boundary confusion in which patients lose their understanding of interior and exterior and the meaning of the "membrane" that divides the two different areas. Thus, one part of the face may be used to create another face, or a body may be drawn inside another body. Sometimes faces will be drawn with no contour lines to delineate what is inside and what is outside, and features sprout up in bizarre places (Figure 1.5). Other features commonly found in Alzheimer's-patient productions include "disorganization, distortions, perceptual rotation, overlapping configurations, confused perspective, and incomprehensible work" (Wald, 1986, p. 75) all of which are due to faulty brain function.

EMOTIONAL CHANGES

The decline in memory, language, and perception all result in a general inability to express oneself and share feelings, causing enormous emotional stress, both to the patient and to the caretakers. The patient may become withdrawn and depressed, giving up the attempt to take part in daily life. It is hard to say how much of the depression is a medical symptom of the illness and

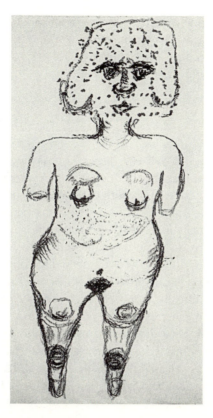

Figure 1.5. Boundary confusion. An armless female figure is initially well formed, but the breasts and pubic area are perceived as eyes and a mouth, turning the torso into a face within a figure. The confusion continues in what seem to be two sets of knees.

how much of it a reaction to the isolation and frustration that results from being ill. The picture is confused because passivity and forgetfulness can theoretically be exacerbated by depression and lack of hope. When the cognitive difficulties are more severe, the patient may become delusional and psychotic, accusing family members of stealing their possessions, of which they themselves cannot keep track. "Who stole my purse" or "Who stole my money?" are constant laments of patients in any daycare center. The functioning of the biological clock gradually deteriorates, so that sleep problems are a common difficulty. Patients tend to roam and wander throughout the night, causing yet more disruptions for the caregivers. Once known to be calm and even-tempered, patients may eventually become aggressive and violent to the point of kicking and punching caregivers as well as strangers. The onslaught of severely faulty brain mechanisms renders the world an unfamiliar place. In the struggle to cope with anger due to increasing losses, patients often turn their hostility onto the people around them.

DISINHIBITION

The appearance of *disinhibition* in the Alzheimer's patient can be extremely unnerving to a caregiver as well as to a therapist. As the dementia proceeds, restraints and inhibitions that have built up over years erode, so that inappropriate impulses cannot be controlled. With the crumbling of more mature defense mechanisms, infantile, unintegrated aspects of the personality are expressed without restraint. Sexually inappropriate behavior is very common among patients where there seems to be no mechanism to judge, and therefore contain, any erotic urge. The greater the deterioration and its concomitant loss of short-term memory, the more the adaptive mechanisms are impaired, leading to less capacity for reality testing, for control of urges, and for self-censorship of criticisms, comments, and general spontaneous aggression. In a sense, a more authentic version of the person emerges, though who is to say if the social personality, developed through the years, is less real than the primitive "true self" which may now be released from critical control. The Alzheimer's patient taking part in an art group cannot be relied on for tactful reflection upon another participant's art productions. The seemingly gentlest of patients can emerge with amazingly cruel, often surprisingly astute observations, without any concern for the feelings of the other.

NARCISSISTIC WORLDVIEW

Another aspect of the advancing disease is the increasingly regressed narcissistic worldview of the Alzheimer's patient. In the developmental process, it takes many years of struggle with separation/individuation issues before the adult develops a mature capacity for compassion for the "other," an ability to conceive of a world seen through the eyes of another. A lifetime of such mature personality structuring begins to unravel as the Alzheimer's patient regresses and becomes more self-involved and incapable of understanding that his needs are not at the center of everyone's world. There is a general eroding of boundaries, similar to that found in the infant. It is as though the skin or membrane separating self and others is gradually eliminated, returning the aged patient to his early, unprotected position. Confused patients can be seen at the dining-room table arguing about their chairs being usurped by someone else, with the total unreasonableness of a toddler. No explanation will curb their rage and determination to get what they want. For the most part, neither explanations nor attempts at compromise solve the problem. Naomi Feil (1993), in her book *The Validation Breakthrough*, provides simple techniques that are useful for dealing with such situations, because they validate feelings rather than focusing on the specific confusion and attempting to objectify the problem. During the therapy hour itself, there is much opportunity for conflict, and the atmosphere often heats up with emotional undercurrents; jealousy of each other's pictures, competitiveness for the therapist's attentions, and paranoia about disappearing works all raise the level of argumentativeness.

One proud and somewhat arrogant elderly woman noticed that another member of the group was drawing from the same journal picture as she had chosen. This put her in a rage similar to that of children in the latency period who complain bitterly that someone is copying from them, as though something is being stolen away from them. In attempting to solve the problem, I showed the group reproductions of the art masters, explaining that "copying" is a form of inspiration, one that Matisse and Picasso made great use of. I talked about interpretation, variation, and generosity, and about imitation as a compliment. Nothing succeeded in calming her, and she raged on, interrupting the quiet work of other members of the group. At moments such as these, carers of Alzheimer's patients have to face the painful fact that there are many times when one is dealing with a child, even if at others they display adult versions of themselves. The more helpful approach is to give up on objective solutions and resort to the very useful validation techniques developed by Naomi Feil (1993), based on the notion that there is a reason behind all behavior and the "empathic listener . . . does not judge them, but accepts their view of reality" (p. 26). Care is taken to mirror the emotional distress and to validate the feelings of both parties: the indignation and understandable stress of the lady who has lost her specialness, whose emotional territory has been invaded, and the right of the victim of her aggression to paint whatever she chooses with complete freedom.

IMPAIRED SENSES

Most therapists who work with the geriatric population are obviously much younger than their patients. It is easy for the young and the robust to overlook very obvious but prevalent physical limitations that affect the patient's engagement in art. The aged, more often than not, have hearing problems, so that one has to give instructions very loudly, slowly and clearly. Their eyesight is often impaired, so that pictures chosen for them to copy should have clear boundaries, with large and prominent images, in order to avoid compounding their confusion. The general age-appropriate limitations are exacerbated by difficulties with comprehension, and extra care must be given to maximizing the chance that they will hear, see, and understand. I showed an enthusiastic artist/patient some reproductions of Picasso's "late period" portraits on which the images are fragmented and distorted, hoping to introduce an element of fun and humor. Instead of finding them amusing she was outraged by the madness of them. "You can't have one eye here and one eye there," she complained, clearly disturbed by the purposeful and controlled distortion that Picasso used. Her own internal world was too threatened and unstable to be able to enjoy an arbitrary world of illogicalities. I learned to bring pictures that made more sense and didn't add frustration to the already crumbling internal world of my patients.

Alzheimer's disease affects patients' *tempo*, both in absorbing and responding to what is said, which could sometimes be read as lack of comprehension or reluctance and resistance. I learned this from Zara, who sat almost comatose in the dining area of the geriatric unit. She had done some minor but surprisingly expressive copies of journal pictures that she had chosen carefully. Hoping to include her in the art-therapy group, I sat next to her, reminding her what it is we do in the group and how much I would like to have her join us. I hoped to engage her by showing her two of her drawings from previous weeks, pointing out their delicacy and the tenderness they brought out in me. Zara was enormously fat, and her head drooped as though she could no longer hold it up, her jaw slack. She was silent and immobile with a fixed facial expression, and I sat near her a little while longer, hopefully, touching her arm, though I could not help but feel slightly defeated. Certain that she did not want to join the group, and somewhat disappointed, I was about to stand up when she grasped my arm and began pulling. Slowly she heaved herself up, and together we walked, arm in arm, at a snail's pace. She smiled at me, glancing shyly at me out of the corner of her eye, a prettiness and femininity emerging as we accompanied each other to the room. She rewarded herself and me with this picture (Figure 1.6) of a delicate bird, which she painstakingly created out of small, choppy lines, though she was still not quite finished with it when the session was over. I could so easily have given up on her that day. Hurried along by my own time schedule, I could have walked away and assumed that she had not heard me, had not understood me, or had not had the desire to be in the art group. And then I would have missed this little gem of a creation, and she, the opportunity to be engrossed in an activity, delighted by the results, and proud of her abilities.

People with Alzheimer's disease are so often depressed, lethargic, and passive. Living in such a disorganized world, where there is so little on which to anchor oneself, would be enough of an explanation for the change in their

Figure 1.6. Zara's bird. Despite advanced dementia and initial lethargy, the patient created this heavily winged bird, possibly an intimation of her heavy chair-bound body.

emotional life. Why would one want to initiate anything when everything is becoming less familiar, when one muddles one's words, when others take over before one has had time to seek one's own appropriate response? And how could one not be paranoid when important items disappear inexplicably or when one is greeted with a hug by someone who appears to be a complete stranger? I sometimes imagine finding myself center stage in a massive operatic production being performed in an unknown language. In this terrifying nightmare, no one can define my role for me—everyone is busy, doing, coming, going, and talking a language I don't comprehend. I can find no place for myself, no order, and no sense. How is it possible to not feel depressed and paranoid?

Throughout the book we will see that the Alzheimer's patient is in a process of losing parts of himself. What he needs is help from the world around to maintain a connection with what he once was, give up what is irretrievably lost, and sustain what he still is. He cannot do it on his own. The danger is that he will be abandoned very soon after he is diagnosed, and all that he was will be whittled down to a classification and a number designated by a test. The surprisingly rich works of many dementia patients provide a strong, contrasting picture to that of their test scores or to the image of them dozing or sitting unenthusiastically, vacantly, and unoccupied in the large common room of a daycare center. As David Shenk (2001) says, "[W]hile medical science gives us tools for staying alive, it cannot help us with the art of living—or dying. . . . With Alzheimer's disease, the caregiver's challenge is to escape the medical confines of *disease* and to assemble a new humanity in the loss" (p. 93). In Michael Ignatieff's novel *Scar Tissue* (1994), the protagonist, who watches his mother's gradual deterioration into advancing dementia, indignantly tells the doctor. "You keep telling me what has been lost, and I keep telling you something remains" (p. 58). Indeed, the art therapist will have to keep track of both. Not until very late into the illness can it be said of the person with Alzheimer's that he is an absence. In many ways, he is more like a lost child, deprived of the mechanisms with which to navigate independently through life. He cannot rely on himself anymore. It behooves us as therapists to understand as much as possible the way the world is now experienced by our patient so as to help him live as full and rich a life as possible, for as long as possible.

2

✳

DOES ART THERAPY REALLY HELP?

Art therapists, faced with the inevitable progression of Alzheimer's disease, and it's accompanying despair, contend with periodic doubts about the real benefits of the therapy they provide. To counter such doubts, it is important to articulate the contribution art therapy makes to those lucky enough to have access to it, even while acknowledging the limitations of the work imposed by dementia. When working with any severely challenged population, therapists themselves must sustain the conviction that what they do is valuable. Oliver Sacks (1985), in writing of a different syndrome, but one in which there is a similar severe loss of memory, considers the dilemma of whether "one could speak of an 'existence', given so absolute a privation of memory or continuity," a world of "isolated impressions" (p. 28). He takes courage from the writings of the great neurologist A. R. Luria, who said, "Man does not consist of memory alone. He has feeling, will, sensibilities, moral being. . . . Neuropsychologically, there is little or nothing you can do; but in the realm of the Individual, there may be much you can do"(p. 32). We should not allow the onslaught of doubt, from the surrounding therapeutic milieu as well as from the therapist's own uncertainties, to undermine the value of the work. All of us need to know that we are heard, seen, responded to, and valued, and we thrive when we inhabit a world that provides us with these experiences. Therapists, no less than any other professionals, need to believe that their investment is meaningful.

It is hard to come to terms with the fact that inevitably the patient is going to deteriorate, even during the period of the therapeutic encounter, if it continues for an extended period. Faced with patients whose world so often has ceased making sense, for whom meaning is often lost, whose stories have neither beginnings nor endings, the therapist is in danger of undermining the significance of his own therapeutic contribution. How does it help? is the question I will try and answer in what follows, with clinical examples of the manner in which art therapy has been significant for Alzheimer's patients.

The necessity for a sense of significance and meaning permeates the therapeutic relationship. The Freudian view of the therapist was of an objective observer of the patient—the therapist as surgeon or archeologist. Not so Heinz Kohut, father of self psychology, who believed that both patient and therapist are providing deep satisfactions, one to the other, without which therapy becomes a dry intellectual endeavor. So at the same time that the patient is being confirmed and validated by the therapist's compassionate presence, the therapist is being sustained by the sense that he is contributing to the well-being of those he works with.

THERAPY OF THE PRESENT

The therapist facilitates an emotional event in the here and now, without hoping to cure or create changes in the internal world of the patient. Art therapy tries to improve quality of life even in people with severely diminished abilities, and to maintain, sustain, and support current capacities. The art therapist witnesses a patient who is invested in a creative project, struggling to organize a world of images on the page. The difficulties and doubts seep in when, minutes later, it becomes clear to the therapist that the patient has no conscious recollection of the entire experience. The perfectly natural need of a therapist to heal and to aim for serious changes in the future must be relinquished for more minor and temporary satisfactions restricted to the present.

An important clarification needs to be made regarding the healing aspects referred to in much of the dialogue regarding art therapy with Alzheimer's. The *American Heritage Dictionary of the English Language*, eighth edition, defines *healing* as "to restore to health; cure" or "to set right; amend" or "to become whole and sound; return to health." Such "healing" implies an altered future. Art therapy with Alzheimer's cannot heal or restore because even as one is working with the patient, the disease is irrevocably causing more damage. It is, however, a therapy, in that it is a *treatment* of physical, mental, or social disorders. It enhances creativity, a very crucial aspect of vital living that through ignorance, neglect, or defeat by hopelessness is in danger of seeming unworthy of investment. Personal expression, increased self worth, and the harnessing of existing abilities, are some of the therapeutic gains that art therapy can bring to its Alzheimer's patients. Unleashing the unconscious processes in order to permit their expression would in itself be a worthwhile endeavor when the alternative for many Alzheimer's patients is passive, almost catatonic inactivity. But more than that can be hoped for. Given art materials and the guidance of a therapist who provides a structure and support, the patient has the opportunity to muster up and make use of remaining internal strengths and ego capacities that provide a series of experiences of competence, mastery, and self-worth.

FREEDOM AND SPONTANEITY

Art therapy aims to provide a spontaneous experience in people whose lives are becoming more rigid, static, and passive. That they are still able to experience such moments of gratification is demonstrated by each small choice they are able and encouraged to make, from the color they choose to draw or paint with, to the images of personal significance to which they choose to return. Paradoxically, it is the very structure of the therapy situation that facilitates greater freedom of expression. "Frames," says Joy Schaverien (1992) "by the fact of their rigidity, provide a complement to, and even facilitate, a certain freedom or opening of the space within"(p. 71). This structure is created concretely, in the form of the repetitive weekly meetings in the increasingly familiar environment of the art room. The therapist greets the patient warmly and opens and closes the session with certain chosen rituals, such as repeating the name of each participant or pointing out pictures they created on a previous occasion. Schaverien talks of this framed space as "a vessel" in which the patient can "explore, play, and experiment"(p. 65). In working with people who are suffering from boundary confusion due to decline in mental functioning, therapists will do well to suggest certain projects, assist with technical ideas, set up a still life, or provide pictures from which to copy. Such structure in a more robust population may inhibit creative vitality, but in an intellectually challenged population it has the effect of instilling a sense of security and safety, providing boundaries within which they can feel the security necessary to take creative risks.

For Esther, a woman in the very early stages of Alzheimer's, providing a concrete frame for the work was crucial in freeing creative courage. To embark on a self-initiated act was far too daring for a woman whose life experience had instilled in her the value of submission, conciliation, and obedience, the very opposite qualities of those needed for creativity. She refused to make a single decision on her own, standing at the threshold of the room and pleading that she didn't know what she was supposed to do. Presented with an empty page and the choice of what she should put on it, she became a little girl, begging permission for her every move. Since she was only mildly cognitively impaired, I found her intensely childish dependence annoying and internally resorted to accusing her of "manipulative and resistant behavior."

Only after I learned of her experience in World War II Europe of being an orphaned Jewish child placed in the strict, puritanical, and cold environment of a Catholic institution did I begin to understand that for her, total obedience to an authoritative voice was a means of survival. Her behavior, in the context of past traumas, the internal emotional logic of it now revealed with clarity, helped me orchestrate a different approach. What I understood to be a liberating opportunity to choose and fulfill her desire was for her a dangerous trap.

Relinquishing the attempt to fight her old childhood pattern, I found a way to take part in it, and in so doing could actually free her somewhat as I adapted to her existential need. Each page that I now presented to her had been prepared in advance with a photocopied frame around the edges of the page. Though in many ways this conflicted with my beliefs about the role of the art therapist, I proceeded to tell her exactly what *I wanted* her to put in the picture, freeing her from the taboo of *her* desires and therefore paradoxically enabling her, at least in part, to follow them. I also provided contour drawings that I invited her to complete; outlines of houses, human figures, and various other objects. Presented with the form of a vase, for instance, she was freed to fill it with flowers, adding colorful decorative elements to it as she worked with obvious pleasure. When I provided the outline of a face, she would willingly complete this with features, as well as investing in a colorfully decorated background (Figure 2.1). Instructions and limitations that for me connote restriction were precisely what she needed in order to invest in any spontaneous, creative act. It is likely that the cognitive and perceptual deterioration of the disease itself was increasing her sense of confused boundaries, leading to a greater need for containers, frames, and shields. However, this fairly universal characteristic of the illness was exacerbated by a particular personality structure, formed in childhood, without knowledge of which the therapist was in danger of becoming rigid and judgmental, thus stifling her capacities.

Esther's life experiences had forced her to find a way to protect herself to the point of isolation, within the boundaries of a frozen emotional world based mostly on compliance with the needs of others and controlled through compulsive organized behavior. What was born out of a need to survive through an unbearably damaging childhood became part of a defensive personality structure in which she was imprisoned. By providing her with this much-needed structure, taking on a motherly role of protection and support, I could, at least for the duration of the art session, allow her to give up part of that self-imposed control and give her permission of sorts to experiment and play, with a certain amount of spontaneity, within the "protected" territory of the page.

Figure 2.1. Filling in contours. Provided with prepared contour drawings, the artist/patient was freed to fill in facial features and add decorative elements around the lines.

As can be seen in Figure 2.2, she invested care and time in the construction of a symbolic protective layer of "skin," the very act of which must have provided an experience of security. On another occasion, presented with the cutout shape of a bird, the patient colored it and accentuated the prepared border with decorative elements (Figure 2.3).

CALMING THE AGITATED PATIENT

Agitation and restlessness are major problems with Alzheimer's patients. As they pace and worry they are unable to disconnect themselves from a loop of

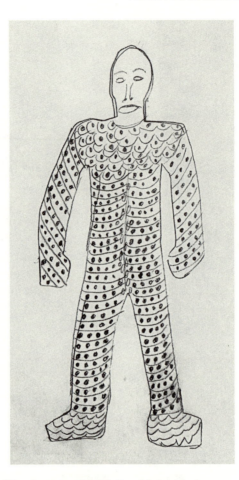

Figure 2.2. The human shield. Provided with the contour of a figure, the patient painstakingly divided it with lines and dots, creating what looks like a protective shield or the carapace of a tortoise.

paranoid thoughts and obsessive behavior. This exhausting—to both patient and caretakers—perseverative behavior prevents them from taking an interest in any other activities. Making the transition from one thought process and emotional state to another becomes more problematic, and patients are capable of repeating the same questions endlessly. The art therapist can guide them to more constructive creative activities, such as painting and sculpting, in order to help them dislocate themselves from previous worrying and refocus on something more enjoyable.

Many patients can make the switch to a creative mode if given the correct

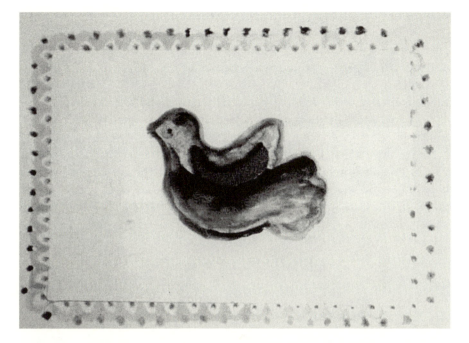

Figure 2.3. A bird in a frame. When the therapist prepared a frame on the page, the patient was freed to create a colorful bird.

guidance. A few brightly colored magazines, a box of cuttings from journals, a flower in a very simple vase, a lump of clay—each can bring about an hour of concentrated pleasure. However, faced with the very resistant patient who refuses to participate, I sometimes suggest that they simply watch me as I paint. If I dip a wide brush into a jar of intense red gouache and make a swirling mark on the page, it often elicits the desire to continue the work I have initiated, and the patient then adds her own color, watching it blend with mine. This is, in itself, a way of commencing a relationship in which our chosen colors, merging on the page, symbolically represent either closeness and harmony or conflict and rejection. The patient who takes up a brush in response to my red markings and smears black paint all over the page is making a very strong and different statement from the patient who dips his brush into pink paint and draws a line close to, and maybe touching, my initial stroke.

Jake, who was severely demented, spent most of his time pacing, staring out the window, approaching and then avoiding the table of art materials, returning to the window to smoke, bursting with restless energy for which he could find no outlet. Seemingly by chance one day, he chose a very small format on which he began to draw with colored crayons. This miniature page, of a size that I had not thought to offer him, enabled him to produce with quiet enthusiasm, his intimate drawings. Judging from his pacing, one could have thought he needed more space, when in fact, his response to the restrictions of the page indicated that it was precisely the security of confinement and containment that he needed in order to calm down. The first picture he chose was of a dog, and for almost an hour, he diligently attempted to reproduce it using colored pencil crayons (Figure 2.4).

His picture is a marked distortion of the original, but the experience served to focus his attention on a pleasant challenge and gave him an opportunity to utilize otherwise uncontained energy. From then on, Jake was a regular in the group, in which he found a resting place where he could peacefully fill his pages with the utmost diligence.

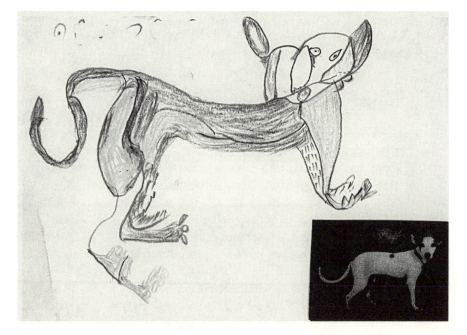

Figure 2.4. Copy of a dog. Despite the distortions, the attempt to copy a photograph of a dog (inset) was sufficiently successful to cause the surprised patient to smile with satisfaction at the result.

THE POWER OF COLOR

The aesthetic immediacy of color talks to the senses in a deep and mysterious manner, affecting a person in a primal direct way, "below the level of rational thought" (Samuels & Samuels, 1975, p. 93). Since this immediacy has little to do with the rational brain, it is more slowly affected by the cognitive decline of Alzheimer's. Michele Cassou (2001) recalls a childhood memory of seeing twenty-four colors displayed on a painting table and instantly hating the green and pink. "They felt so ugly. To be so strongly repelled by colors is proof of how deeply they affected me. . . . At other times, I would love colors so much that I couldn't help but touch them with my fingers and paint with them. Sometimes I wished I could have eaten the colors!"(p. 218). Making use of this powerful, visceral attraction and repulsion toward certain colors, an art therapist can facilitate many creative encounters. According to Schachtel (1959) (Samuels & Samuels, 1975), color is not only "recognized, but is felt as exciting or soothing, dissonant or harmonious, joyous or somber, warm or cool, disturbing and distracting or conducive to concentration and tranquility" (p. 93). Color not only affects mood or mind states but actually affects the body directly. Gerard (Samuels & Samuels, 1975) studied the effects of color on human physiology and found that blood pressure, electric conductance of the skin, respiration rate, eye blinks, and brain wave patterns were affected significantly differently when a person was exposed to the color red as opposed to blue. None of these physiological influences has been studied directly with Alzheimer's patients; however, my experience has taught me to be aware of, and use my intuition regarding, the powerful effects of specific colors on each individual patient while painting. When working, for instance, with a particularly resistant patient who might be seriously impaired, passive, or very depressed, a session may involve inviting him to choose a color out of a box of oil pastels. I, too, might then choose one and make a colored shape on the page, inviting the patient to add his shape or line. With a severely depressed person, I might choose a strong, deep red, hoping that the intensity will arouse a response. A timid or anxious patient might find such intense color overwhelming, and I would therefore introduce a more calming, pastel color. Such work, begun by simply playing with the color itself and its effect on the page, is enough to facilitate a lively experience for the patient, often resulting in a large rainbow picture, or a colorful page of shapes and lines. Making use of the natural attraction and repulsion towards certain colors, the art therapist can facilitate many creative encounters. A palette of freshly poured colored paints presented to the Alzheimer's patient can be a seductive invitation to dip into and create forms on the page. A brightly colored art reproduction can be a strong stimulus for the patient to try and adopt some of the colors for his own artistic creations in a similar way. One such lady, frustrated and isolated by her total aphasia and profound confusion, spent many hours filling pages with colorful patterns. Her primitive but colorful renditions of trees, animals, and human figures delighted both her and the visitors to the exhibition of her work after a year of participation in the art-therapy group.

THE POWER OF CHOICE: FOSTERING INDEPENDENT ACTIVITY

Dementia patients face a rapid decline in capabilities that inevitably eats away at ego strength and deeply affects self-esteem. The evidence provided by a patient's artwork challenges his gradually diminishing self-esteem and powerlessness, providing concrete confirmation of his existing energy and potential for creative self-expression. One of the many noted symptoms of the early stages of the disease is the growing difficulty in making personal choices. Because of the confused perceptions and lack of judgment, the patient struggles when weighing options. Confidence is diminished, and patients appeal to others to take charge of and control over what are experienced as emotionally overwhelming situations. Although this increasing dependence and relinquishing of authority is due in part to failing mental functioning, it is exacerbated by the natural tendency for caretaker figures to assist and make decisions for the patient. As with other disabled people, many tasks dementia patients may be capable of undertaking are whipped away from them by more competent people, which compounds their marginalization from life.

Given compassionate support and time to process and respond to information, the patient himself would often be capable of making certain decisions and acting on them, instead of which, all autonomous behavior is gradually diminished. Jane Harlan (1990) highlights the stress that mental-health literature puts on *management* of the patient, as opposed to interventions such as art therapy where "promoting aspects of the older individual's *autonomy* becomes particularly challenging and complex" (p. 99). Whatever can be done to provide opportunities for the Alzheimer's sufferer to make personal decisions, acts that come out of an inner impulse, should be encouraged. "Our dismay as we witness others literally losing their minds may lead us to overprotect them as a way of protecting ourselves from the frightening specter of our own inevitable losses" (Harlan, 1990, p. 99). The danger is that in witnessing this self-determination and purposeful activity being stripped away by the disease, the caretaker, instead of supporting and motivating may, in trying to help, be "demeaning and constricting"(p.99). At the very least, engaging a person in choosing an image of their liking, providing a color that pleases them, or in fact any form of choice encouraged in the artistic endeavor, will add up to personal expression and spontaneous activities that are the basic ingredients of a sense of self-worth.

It would be hard to express with anyone other than my colleagues at work the joy I have sometimes felt when a severely demented patient has rejected my choice of a color and insisted on her own instead or, when I've observed a seemingly vacant and unresponsive patient slide a page toward himself and commence copying a picture of his choice. Once one's expectations have been realistically lowered, these small acts of independence are very meaningful. Though many patients in a geriatric facility do not remember the art room from one meeting to another, clearly there is some recollection at an experiential level, which can be seen in the growing comfort and familiarity with the art materials when they enter the art room. When patients see work they have done, even moments after its creation, they often greet it with a surprised, "I did that?" after which comes the pride and respect of, "That's very nice!"

In some fairly rare instances, the patient will continue to create art away from the session, both resulting from and increasing a sense of independence and power. The art objects then function as forms of transitional objects, the equivalent of the toddler's calming teddy bear, connecting them with the loving mother/therapist, even when she is not present. Ofra Kamar (1997) was the therapist of an extremely isolated patient "imprisoned in [his] own world, unable to communicate with or relate to others." In weekly group meetings, he began to connect several dots that the therapist drew on a page, and out of these he created complex creatures, which the therapist concluded were an expression of his fears and anxieties. With the encouragement of his wife, he continued to create his creatures at home, in a way that reduced "his tension, isolation and frustration" (p. 123). I was gratified in a similar way when, after the death of a patient to whom I had felt particularly connected, I paid a condolence visit to his wife, seeking closure for myself after a meaningful relationship of some years. She showed me the dozens of pictures that he had drawn each day on his return from the unit. "He came home, ate his lunch and went to his table to draw. It was one of the only things left which interested him," she told me. The quality of the pictures was somewhat inferior to those done within the confines of the art therapy group. They were hastily executed and were more repetitious, but they were pictures he had chosen to do independently, without the presence of the therapist. Clearly, these dozens of pictures that he left behind had acquired an important consoling function in his increasingly empty existence, connecting him to the positive experience he had during our meetings.

ASSISTING THE CAREGIVERS

When art therapists work with troubled children, they take on board the task of interpreting the child's internal world through the artwork and communicating to the parents what can be gleaned in order to assist them in understanding and handling their children's difficulties. This bridging function becomes an important part of the therapy itself. So, too, the art therapist working with Alzheimer's patients can sometimes use the art products to help burdened caregivers understand the inner world of their loved ones. It is expecting too much from the caregiver who is exposed daily to the endless questions and unstable emotional condition of the stricken family member to sustain the patience and calm presence that a professional worker can provide. Whereas the therapist might find meaning in often-garbled communications, a patient is often lost to his family, who feel that the person they once knew has all but vanished. Abigail had spent many of her therapy sessions drawing intimate scenes of simple daily activities, to which she added short lines of explanation. Gradually the proportion of text to images changed, until she finally gave up drawing, choosing instead to compose stories based on photographs and pictures that I provided each week. After two years of working in this way, I compiled all of these into a bound book and invited her daughters and other family members to a "reading." Abigail had to be reminded every so often that she was the author of these stories that clearly impressed her as she listened to them and that it was because of her that we had all gathered together. Her teary-eyed daughters were amazed to listen to the touching fragments, written in an expressive language by a mother who, by this time, they could only see as a sad dementia sufferer with nothing to say.

Inspired by a reproduction of a painting of a male figure with a small house in the background, Abigail wrote:

> The house is empty—all have gone
> He is left alone, bereft, no connection with anyone.
> He looks around. Searches for someone.
> Someone familiar from the past . . . there is no-one
> Even his glance is uncertain
> As though asking for an answer to it
> Who should I turn to? wonders the youth.

> As though he asks for a solution from someone
> Who will answer him—now the house is empty?

In fragments such as these, she is clearly identifying with the "bereft" youth, alone in an empty house. In this metaphorical piece she is expressing the emptiness of her own inner house, her world that has slowly been emptied of life. Through the poem, Abigail's family could gain a deeper understanding of the sense of abandonment and longing of their practically mute mother.

VALUE OF GROUP EXPERIENCE

Group art-therapy experiences provide rewards of their own that are often more suitable for Alzheimer's patients than one-on-one encounters are. The latter can be important when patients first join a center, in order to develop initial trust, reduce the anxiety of engaging with art materials, and as a way to familiarize themselves with the therapist as she helps them adapt to the new setting of the unit they are attending. Ultimately, however, much is gained from repeated meetings with familiar group members with whom they can experience a common activity. Such group encounters can somewhat alleviate the personal isolation through the camaraderie of a social interactive group. Simon (see Chapter 5), for instance, quickly became an enthusiastic and important member of the art-therapy group. He was a particularly positive presence, responding to the art of the other participants with unusual insight and compassion, providing relevant and encouraging feedback. This gave him an opportunity to be "the helper," a role that provided him with new reserves of self-esteem.

In the context of the community of the group, a wide range of emotional interaction is elicited, not always positive, but often lively and competitive, the negative price of which can be a display of envy and nastiness. Patients suffering from "disinhibition" do not have adequate social judgment, nor are they sufficiently in control to hide socially unacceptable behavior. The risk of asking for any feedback on the artwork of fellow members of the group is that patients will criticize mercilessly, without regard for the hurt of the "other." Their world has become far more egocentric, with rules of social conduct slipping away as more infantile selfishness is released. The therapist might permit the expression of some of the hostility and competitiveness that will be aroused but should watch out for the more vulnerable members of the group and protect them. These might be people who are by nature more sensitive to criticism, or those in the early stages of dementia who are more likely to be offended because they are still more aware of the significance of negativity from those around them.

In a group one finds a source of stimulation and creative energy that is lacking within the intimate patient/therapist dyad. When interacting in a group, participants can actually use each other as a source of ideas for their creative work by copying the colors that a neighbor is using, feeling freer to use a material they hadn't thought about before, or copying from the same picture as another participant. One of the more skilled patients in one group meeting created an impressive picture of a tranquil scene in which two people are sitting in a boat on a river, surrounded by meadows that could be confused with choppy water (Figure 2.5). Not surprisingly, this well-articulated work attracted the attention of the other participants, who tried their hand at the same task, and though they were far less adept, some managed to reconstruct this scene of intimacy, togetherness, and friendship. Yet another participant wanted to copy the boat scene but made serious changes to the original picture (Figure 2.6). While he managed to produce a picture of a man rowing, he eliminated the second figure, creating a boatman alone in the scene, which conveys a very different atmosphere from that of the other pictures, one that probably gives voice to his loneliness.

Figure 2.5. Boat scene, 1. A patient chooses a picture and skillfully copies the content.

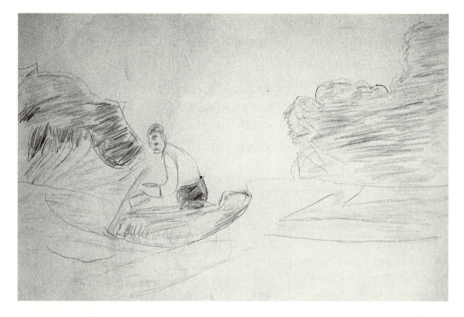

Figure 2.6. Boat scene, 2. In this attempt to copy the scene in Figure 2.5, the changes that the artist made evoke solitariness rather than the camaraderie of a couple in the original.

Sometimes a group theme can elicit unexpected responses as each patient is enlivened by the contribution of the other participants. In one such meeting, after the patients had produced their images connected with the mother/child theme, the therapist hung up a blank paper and asked each member to say something in response to the various pictures. Words were tossed about, sentences struggled to be born, and associations of any kind were accepted and jotted down.

THE LOVE OF A MOTHER

"Mother and child—it is the whole world"

"To be happy, to see mother hug the child"

"From joy, tears come to her eyes"

"The mother feels warmth"

"Lets the child drink from her breast or her body"

"Maybe they went out to dance from joy"

"When you will be big, when there is no more war"

"When you will grow up peacefully"

"When you will have a good life"

"When you will be healthy"

"The child feels warmth in the arms of its mother"

"He feels connection and warmth"

"A close hug—he feels love in his heart"

"The mother says—don't be afraid, child, everything will come out well"

"Devotion and unending love"

Many of these sentences came from participants who speak with great difficulty, yet the emotional connection with the task compensated for some of this muteness, stimulated memories, and provided the extra impetus to communicate. For people increasingly deprived of social interaction, such experiences are extremely gratifying, and release unexpected vitality.

ART THERAPY AS AN ADJUNCTIVE DIAGNOSTIC MEASURE

Alzheimer's disease cannot be definitively diagnosed without a biopsy (the removal and examination of brain tissue—which is considered a pointless surgical invasion). Since there is currently no curative treatment, it would make no sense to endanger a patient with such a procedure. One can only talk of probable Alzheimer's after excluding other illnesses such as multi-infarct dementia, brain tumors, Parkinsonian dementia, and others. There is a battery of fairly simple very successful standard diagnostic tests available that indicate whether or not a person is suffering from Alzheimer's disease—the Mini Mental State Examination. Artwork itself can provide useful additional information regarding deficits and remaining capacities. Judith Wald (1983) suggests asking patients to draw certain subjects: a self-portrait, a person sitting across the table, a face, a house, and a simple still life. This, she finds, yields information about the effects of the disease on mental capacities and also taps into the patients' emotional reactions to their health situations. In a later paper, Wald (1986) describes the characteristics of Alzheimer's art as including "regression, perseveration, simplification, fragmentation, disorganization and distortions, perceptual rotation, overlapping configurations, confused perspective and incomprehensible work" (p. 75). Kathleen Kahn-Denis (1997) describes the more common elements in the graphic representations of Alzheimer's patients that indicate organic changes in the brain: the presence of short, scattered lines; perseveration, such as in the constant repetition of lines, shapes, or symbols; a small, cramped appearance; disconnections from drawing to drawing; impoverishment, in which essential features are omitted; difficulty in following instructions; and attention deficits such as the failure to integrate separate features into a coherent whole. The presence of these features can also help to distinguish the organicity of Alzheimer's disease, as opposed to treatable dementias such as in depression or delirium. Kahn-Denis illustrates the contribution that the art diagnosis can make, through the work of an 82-year-old woman with Alzheimer's over a two year period, in which one can see the progressive fragmentation of line quality, increasing perseveration, and gradual disappearance of form. This particular woman retained her social persona while the art was being done, and this masked the significant losses of cognitive abilities, which were more clearly displayed in these graphic qualities. This was useful information for the staff, because it was a call for more supportive services in spite of her unchanging social facade. "The art productions seem to graphically mimic the course of a progressive dementia, in a sense a type of handmade x-ray reflecting the cognitive experience of the individual with dementia" (Kahn-Denis, 1997, p. 195). In a similar way, the art of Willem de Kooning demonstrates many of the depletions of the disease as they affected his functioning. In the last pictures of his life, the swirling lines and bands of color are reminiscent of the structural lines of his early paintings, except that they are increasingly empty, showing a loss of the layered complexity of those earlier works and, unfortunately, of his mind.

ART AS A MEANS OF REMINISCING

By jolting the memory through sensory stimuli of various sorts, one can facilitate reminiscing, returning and connecting to the past, so that the sense of continuity of self can be affirmed. Unpublished research by Debbie Lahav and Tsippie Vainer Benaiah (1998) indicates that Alzheimer's sufferers retain a premorbid (i.e., before onset of illness) self-image even though, as it becomes clear when family members are interviewed, they have changed markedly. If they were to lose that subjective sense of a continuing self, they would lose one of the few anchors still available to them. Reminiscing helps them retain this connection to the past that becomes more significant as short-term memory evades them. It could be said that the Alzheimer's patient lives largely in the past, because this is where most of his more established memories reside, providing a more stable source of sustenance. It is in that place of long ago that one should actually set out to meet him. The therapist can bring in artifacts and vintage objects from the period and culture of the patients' youth, such as hats and headwear worn when the patient was growing up, or old pots, pans, and crockery, or books that he might have been exposed to as a child. Period photographs often bring a sparkle of life to the otherwise passive and disconnected patient as he recognizes familiar forms and faces. All these have the power to awaken snippets of memories that are so confirming to a person gradually losing a sense of location, relationships, and past connections. Abigail, who chose pictures from magazines and then wrote stories inspired by them, kept returning to her very intense memories of life as a young woman, when, as an immigrant, she had faced uncertainty, war, and the challenges of learning a foreign language. Although she barely talked about her current family, these early experiences became the subject of many of her stories, which focused on young women who longed for love, lived lives of loneliness, and faced life's hardships.

Angela Byers (1995) talks about the frustration of working with patients with severe memory loss, from whom "thoughts disappear from consciousness so quickly that the logical sequence of normal thinking cannot be maintained" (p. 13). However, though the brain cannot find the right words to describe them, there are many fragments of long-term memory that are still intact. Feelings, though they come and go swiftly, can be extremely intense. She failed in her attempt to engage her patients in any true art-therapy process, but she did observe, and then encouraged them, in activities of arranging and playing with an assortment of materials. Instead of discarding this as random rearranging of the objects, she saw that they had quite significant meaning for the patients, some of which was due to the triggering of old memories.

ART AS A MEANS TO EXPRESSING EMOTIONS

As verbal skills deteriorate, Alzheimer's sufferers are increasingly deprived of a language through which to express their feelings, deepening their isolation and depression. Art activities provide a nonverbal means for touching on feelings and communicating them to those who would be concerned with relating to their content. Enhancing emotional expression in a therapeutic context can affect a patient's state in a variety of ways. On the one hand, it can serve as a life-affirming, pleasant activity that distracts the patient from distress and sadness, and on the other, it can touch off painful and uncomfortable emotions, providing a legitimate outlet for them. There is a controversy regarding the extent to which therapists should guide patients to more expressive work and thus risk the upheaval of pain and despair and the possible consequent internal disorganization. There are therapists who incline toward a policy of resignation and suppression, preferring to provide an hour of pleasurable experiences. This dilemma must be resolved by each therapist, according to his own personal therapeutic conceptions but also taking into account the ego strength of a particular patient, the extent of damage caused by the disease, and respect for the patient's desire to share or reticence about his inner world. Therapeutic styles are influenced by the unconscious inclinations of the therapist; some want to avoid painful issues, fearing their own despair as well as that of their patients', whereas others are personally opposed to the soothing aspects of art activities and want to encourage more cathartic emotional experiences.

Phyllis Jarvinen and Steven Gold (1979) point to the power of "nondepressive daydreams" (p. 523) as an aid to reducing depression. Since depression occurs in 20 percent of people with Alzheimer's disease, providing them with positive experiences might have beneficial effects. For certain patients who have tendencies to dwell on repetitive negative themes, such as guilt, self-criticism, and dependence, it could be beneficial to direct them to more positive subjects, optimistic themes, and pleasant memories to reduce their depression. There are patients for whom touching on painful material will be so unhinging that they might even leave the room or act out their distress in angry outbursts. Yet, for others, pleasant creative activities might ultimately be unsatisfying, depriving them of the opportunity to give voice to their worries and gripes which could be expressed in their art productions.

Therapists often have to contend with pervasive anger that dementia patients experience as a result of the decline in their capacities, helplessness, changes in living spaces, loss of prestige, and exclusion from relationships. Often the anger arises because objects are misplaced and it is too painful to face the fact that the disappearance is actually due to their own failing memory. Finding such an explanation unacceptable, they resort to the paranoid belief that things have been stolen or removed by hostile forces. Over time, caretakers run out of the patience needed to listen to the harping anger and unjustified accusations. Some of this patient's anger and frustration can be released on a piece of paper or by working with clay.

ART AS A MEANS OF ACCESSING STRENGTHS

From the moment a patient is diagnosed with Alzheimer's and then allocated a label and a numerical value on a scale of deterioration, it is as though he has dropped from one category of existence to another; as though there is no "terrain that lies between *healthy* and *demented*" (Shenk, 2001, p. 32). In fact, this is not necessarily a true reflection of reality. The range of functioning between health and ill health, between sound and failing memory, between self-awareness and oblivion is wide. Earlier diagnosis means that there are more years during which the person can continue to benefit from enrichment programs and any creative means that access remaining lively capabilities. Cancer patients tell of the significance of the ways in which the community responds once the dreaded diagnosis is made public—that the person with cancer often feels marginalized and no longer a part of the mainstream. Oliver Sacks writes, "Our tests . . . our 'evaluations,' are ridiculously inadequate. They only show us deficits, they do not show us powers; they only show us puzzles and schemata, when we need to see music, narrative, play" (1985, p. 172).

You will often see colleagues in units such as ours sharing, with excitement and enthusiasm, a scribble from a formerly extremely lethargic patient or a lively comment from a severely aphasic woman. For us it is a small miracle when a hyperactive patient manages to concentrate for long enough to create a symmetrical clay pot that somehow manages to hold together or when a depressed patient shouts out one's name in the corridor and says, "Good to see you." According to Sacks (1985), the dangers of psychological testing are that they "decompose . . . into functions and deficits" (p. 172). He describes his meeting with a young woman who had availed herself of a symbolic language, though a disjointed one. "She had come apart horribly in formal testing, but now, when she was provided the opportunity to utilize alternative internal strengths she was mysteriously 'together' and composed" (p. 172). The art therapist concentrates on remaining powers, by addressing that which still functions and attempts to slip past the failing cognitions. He is an optimistic miner who believes there is a chance that within the rubble is buried something that shines and glows and is worth bringing out to the light.

COMMUNICATING THROUGH METAPHORS

One of the ways to compensate for the loss of language skills due to Alzheimer's is to access the potential richness of metaphoric communications. The "capacity to express one thing in terms of another" (Siegelman, 1990, p. 1) in order to communicate an experience is an elementary structure of thought. It is a natural phenomenon of the human mind to think, for example, of disappointment in love as a knife in the heart or of a joyous moment as the sudden emergence of the sun from black clouds. Metaphors exert tremendous power over us, through their vividness, resonance, and connection to the world of sensed and felt experience.

Graced with the ability to express internal psychological realities in a way that direct description cannot, through the use of metaphors, patients can connect, at a feeling level, with the content, yet remain unaware of and unexposed to the underlying threatening significance. The language of metaphors bypasses the censorship of the logical and critical mind, permitting the artist/patient to touch on painful subjects without becoming suspicious or ashamed. For instance, in a drawing, the demon of one's anger can bare its teeth, yet one does not have to become consciously aware of being aggressive. And, if a patient draws a male and female figure strolling together hand in hand, the therapist does not necessarily add much by saying that the patient is longing for connection. The image has already said that, possibly more successfully than words could. Jung (1963), reflecting on the significance of his art activities, said that he "learned how helpful it can be, from the therapeutic point of view, to find the particular image that lies behind the emotions," and, further, that "to the extent that [he] managed to translate the emotions into images" he was "inwardly calmed" (p. 171).

Metaphors have the power to contain conflicting content within them; dialectic material brought together, condensed and united with great precision. Zara's bird (see Figure 1.6) expresses both her unarticulated desire for the lightness of flight and the contradictory reality of the heaviness of her earthbound wings. Both the reality of the restriction of her overweight body, and the longing for greater mobility found a place in the wordless image of the bird. When Esther (see Figure 2.2) covered the body she had drawn with an armor-like pattern, she was driven by the need to protect her crumbling inner self, and at the same time, satisfy her need for control and mastery over her fear. The metaphor functions in such a way that it connects her both with the emotional fragility of her inner world but at the same time, creates a sturdy means to protect her. In so doing, she moves backward and forward between these polar experiences of strength and vulnerability, courage and fear. In the case of Alzheimer's, ordinary words are increasingly unavailable, whereas the image and its metaphorical meaning remain accessible.

There are images that have particular appeal to the Alzheimer's patients, to which they tend to gravitate when given a choice. Vases, pots, and vessels of different sorts are attractive because of their simple shapes and lines. They also have emotional significance as metaphorical containers, places in which to store precious things for safekeeping. Innumerable folk tales and legends contain themes of buried treasure, hidden caskets, and secret containers with jewels, all of which are themselves metaphors for the function of the therapist as a safe place or keeper of the soul. The attraction to the container as an image conveys, in part, the patient's unconscious need for the "containing" aspect of the therapeutic relationship; a longing for an "other" who will take over the task of holding and supporting the patient as he gradually loses the capacity to recompose himself in the face of his growing internal fragmentation.

The tree is an example of a single image that is generally evocative for patients (Plates 1 and 2). Graphically simple to produce with two straight lines for a trunk and a circle for the crown, minimal drawing skills are needed. A tree has the potential to express the fundamental polarities of life and death, growth and decay, power and fragility, and community and isolation. Morris was a permanent member of an art-therapy group for more than two years, during which time he almost exclusively drew and painted trees, regardless of any alternate project I suggested. Practically mute, of a frozen, autistic bearing, and refusing all eye contact, Morris would shuffle into my room and sit passively. Many sessions passed before he dipped his brush into the paint and began the "tree," adventure. For Morris, the tree became a vessel for an array of feeling states which he certainly had no capacity to express verbally and of which he probably was not consciously aware. He painted trees in a group, single trees, trees covered with a crown of green leaves, trees that seemed to be stripped of their greenery and pared down to the bare branches of their being, trees on circular formats, and trees that had lost their containing form and had become lost in their surroundings. In one portrayal the sun is surrounded by a cold band of blue that prevented its potential warmth from reaching the tree that is in the center of the page. It is as if Morris himself is deprived of the warmth of the world around him, though he is aware that it exists somewhere out there. In Figure 2.7, two trees with flexible trunks and bare branches display a fragility reminiscent of the skeletal remains of a fish whose flesh and life have been eliminated, possibly a depiction of Morris's sense of depletion. In one of his later pictures, the crowns of the trees had been discarded and replaced with the phallic forms of the trunks painted in strongly colored reds and oranges.

Morris, sitting silently and rigidly in my room, proved to be the bearer of an inner world that could not have been imagined simply by observing his exterior. A year after his inclusion into the group art-therapy sessions, his psychiatrist rewarded me with a letter describing the startling changes that he observed in this man who had been rendered totally isolated by his illness for the preceding five years. His wife confirmed these observations, surprised that now, after so many years, he had become markedly more communicative. A single image—a tree—served as a metaphor that, his doctor remarked, had opened a channel to the expression of his closed internal life, awakening his interest in others and of the world outside himself. It was almost impossible to engage Morris in any discussion about his creations, and it never seemed very important to do so. The images, imbued with feelings and imagination, spoke for themselves. The words of Rollo May (1975) clarify some of the urgency of these varied depictions of trees. "The creative process is the expression of this passion for form. It is the struggle against disintegration, the struggle to bring into existence new kinds of being that give harmony and integration" (p. 169).

Another image that has universal, symbolic significance with the potential to express complex and contradictory messages is that of the house. For children, a house is the most popular image after that of the human figure and

Figure 2.7. Two bare trees. These wintry trees indicate a sense of loss and impoverishment.

appears in 60 percent of spontaneous drawings. As the child matures, the appearance of the house decreases in frequency, possibly because of the emancipation from dominant familial ties of the earlier years (Di Leo, 1973). It is possible that the image of the house reappears in Alzheimer's in order to express regressive emotional needs, as a result of the narrowing of the sphere of interest, a longing for a sense of security and belonging, and the desire to return to primal relationships. Given this regressive tendency, any house, drawn or sculpted, will be an expression of the early needs of the patient/artist and provide a language through which to render internal realities based on individual histories. The size of the house, its place on the page, the colors and materials chosen, as well as the addition or absence of exterior features will all tell the private story of its creator, in a sense becoming a self-portrait.

If a selection of pictures of houses is offered to patients, the picture he chooses represents aspects that are emotionally meaningful to him, whether he chooses the solitary houses of Edward Hopper or the colorful and lively houses of Friedensreich Hundertwasser. The artist/patient never makes an exact copy but rather makes changes according to his needs. Clara, for instance, chose a picture that has the appearance of a fortress, and indeed, a member of the group declared, "That's not a house. It's just walls," while another scoffed that it looked like a prison. Clara was a secretive and emotionally withdrawn woman, with a quite combative persona. It wasn't surprising that she chose to represent her psyche as a "fortress," constructed to avoid invasion rather than to make a place for the living. In her painting, the house takes on the form of a well-protected domain with thick gray walls and an intense blue sky wrapped around them, providing yet another protective layer.

Simon (Figure 2.8), on the other hand, chose a picture of a colorful and dynamic multileveled domain occupied by figures walking inside and out, but in his interpretation, though the building is colorful and complex, the human figures have been evicted. He said of the work, "A lonely man lives here," dramatizing the split between the potential liveliness of the original picture—and presumably representing his true longing for human contact—and the loneliness of his deserted residence.

Abigail's picture (Figure 2.9) evokes a sense of community. Two houses are connected by a path on which a figure moves from one to the other. Donkeys, chickens, birds, and trees inhabit this lively world of communion, contact, and interaction. After drawing the picture, she composed a story in which she talked in poetic language about "swaying trees . . . the palm tree stretching up to the skies . . . children planting and watering the bushes that will enjoy the fruits of their labor next year." This image and story so successfully capture the strong, optimistic, and vibrant nature of this handsome, elegant woman, who suffered increasingly from the limitations of Alzheimer's but retained a sociable, communicative persona struggling to express itself.

Greta's houses, on the other hand, could never be inhabited by such interaction. These were always placed in the center of the page, without any foundation line, intimating a sense of groundlessness and insecurity. The door is closed and has no path leading to it; dried branches or twigs encroach on the house, isolating it from other parts of the landscape. Greta was extremely arrogant about her drawing skills and very critical of the other members of the group. Her perceived superiority and separateness seem to provide her with a great deal of satisfaction, though the image also shows the isolation and desiccation that are the price of her haughtiness, and her liveliness is strangled by the vines (Figure 2.10). It is because of the power of the metaphor that these polarities can be contained in this one image.

Figure 2.8. The abandoned house. The sense of loneliness is enhanced by the elimination of a number of lively figures, which the artist removed from the original picture that he copied.

The art therapist is advised when working with metaphors to stay with the image, so to speak, in the sense of respecting the creative act as therapeutic in itself, as a cathartic and satisfying event that organizes inner experience, without bringing the material to consciousness. The Alzheimer's patient operates more and more through primary-process thinking, which is dominated by unconscious, associative thought processes. The art therapist is trained to tune into and make sense of this primary process, which is so

Figure 2.9. A busy community. The houses are part of an active world populated by people and animals in movement and communication.

Figure 2.10. An inhospitable house. Deprived of a secure base, the house is engulfed in dried branches that discourage access.

basic to the creative act. He will "listen" to the myth, to the story, to the patient's symbol, with another sort of ear—the third ear, as it were—one that is less concerned with rational views, psychological interpretations, or reductionist explanations.

ART THERAPY AS A SOURCE OF RELATIONSHIPS

Art therapy is first and foremost about relationships; any of the art activities that take place in the therapy room, happen within the framework of a trusting connection. Joy Schaverien (1992) observes that the therapy picture is animated by current feelings, by the content of the relationship in which it was made. Winnicott (1971), who explored the significance of infancy on emotional development, took the mother/child couple as a paradigm of the therapist/patient relationship regarding the mother/baby set-up as central to the future well being of the person. In fact, he could also be describing the therapist/patient dyad. The Alzheimer's patient is gradually deprived of any such "unit," isolated as he is by the increasing invasions of the illness. Imagine the delight, the gift of the presence of an "other" who listens with absolute attention, is present without irritation, is committed to help unravel one's meaning and intentions, guides one to an activity that will touch on personal themes, and tries to give voice to an emotional state that the confused patient cannot access through words. The therapist who is attuned in such a way, who facilitates such an encounter, who is emotionally able to be in such a relationship, is rewarded with surprising, creative gifts as well as enormous gratitude and love.

Ofra Kamar (1997) demonstrated that her presence, and the ensuing relationship, imbued the creative activities with a deeper significance. In her work with a severely agitated and practically mute Alzheimer's patient, she provided as a stimulus, a few dots on a page, which he then spent many sessions and hours connecting, forming them into emotionally charged creatures. But when she was absent from a session, he refused to connect the dots drawn by any other members of the staff. Clearly the relationship with the now absent Kamar was fundamental in catalyzing this creative capacity and drive. It seems that some trust had developed which caused him to feel that Kamar could "see" him in a way that others might not. Just connecting the dots and creating creatures was not enough; the activity was only a part of the pleasure. What he needed was a witness; one who could make sense of, and unravel, his communications. In Kamar's words, "there is no one way to reach an individual. Had it not been for cooperative drawing, Steve's own rich, fascinating world might have remained undiscovered" (1997, p. 123).

Among the pictures and reproductions that I often presented to patients as a means to stimulate and to catalyze artistic activity was a varied collection of images representing the mother/child connection. This popular theme is driven by increasingly regressive needs for the protective mothering presence. These are always pictorially complicated images because one figure has to be fitted within another, hands and feet forming confusing, entangled patterns (Plates 3 and 4). Yet patients regularly gravitated to these images, working on their technically difficult mission with concentrated attention. What emerged was usually a confused result, the original theme often barely discernible in the final product. Yet, this does not detract from what is the driving emotional force behind the choice of an image and dedication to the task. Within the transference relationship we see expressed the longing for early dependence, a desire to be taken care of by the nurturing therapist in a way that evokes the longing for a mother figure. The choice of this difficult image, as well as the drive to struggle with it graphically, indicated the primal memory of the mother caressing and caring for the helpless child. This experience was relived through the choice of the picture of the mother/child dyad, the uninterrupted opportunity to focus on the image, and the caressing of the forms while recreating an experience with repeated pencil lines.

Marion Milner (1969) describes an image that appeared in the work of her patient, of a figure with the head of a baby indicated in cradling arms. "It was poignant, full of anguish, yet also seemed to have in it a faint glimmer of hope," an expression of the "psychic equivalent of the containing arms" (Thomson, 1989, p. 31). Thomson's description of the way in which therapists respond to the "artistry" of the mentally ill is applicable to Alzheimer's patients. "We realize that something about the work may be cramped, one-sided or paper thin, that it may not unfold or flower, and yet we are moved by it. Indeed, as an art therapist it is difficult not to be over impressed by abilities that come to the fore" (p. 39). Art therapists have a natural enthusiasm for any act that comes out of spontaneous volition, especially from patients who one knows have so many limitations imposed by a disease. Maybe it is this enthusiasm that is the equivalent of a mother's gaze that the patient "knows" and that briefly returns to him a sense of his wholeness and worth, driving him to find more reserves so that he can try his hand yet again at creating magic.

3

※

THE THERAPEUTIC HOUR:
A PRACTICAL GUIDE

I wanted the healing process to grow out of the patient's own personality,
not from a suggestion by me that would have only a passing effect.
—Carl Jung

In the drive to facilitate a meaningful creative experience for patients, the therapist has to take into account the particular population with whom he is working, bearing in mind their disabilities as well as their strengths and adapting the skills of his craft to these issues. Less-experienced therapists are often surprised that materials which were so effective in catalyzing creative productions in one group of patients actually managed to overwhelm and even unhinge others. As an example, Florence Cane's (1983) methods of encouraging creativity through scribbles and random marks on paper that then suggest an image for the patient is likely to frustrate the Alzheimer's patient. For a person suffering from dementia, this meeting with a page full of abstract, chaotic lines and colors mimics her own increasingly confused perceptual and cognitive world. Our task is to try and avoid evoking more of this anxiety, increase where possible a sense of order and meaning, and find a supportive, proactive approach to helping patients use whatever internal capacities they still have. This goes for all the therapeutic choices, such as the setting of the room, number of participants, the art materials offered, the specific projects suggested, the therapeutic interventions, and more. In order to promote a sensitive holding environment, the therapist has to take into account "the changing levels of ego integration, defenses, resistances, object representations, and the like. This adds a subtle dimension to a subject that is often treated as a series of recipes for various populations" (Robbins & Goffia-Girasek, 1987, p. 104). In this chapter I will elaborate on the practical challenges of the therapeutic hour, not as a "series of recipes" but as an attempt to match the generic aspects of art therapy with the specific needs of the patient challenged by the advances of dementia.

MATERIALS

The materials that the art therapist makes available to his patients are the ABCs of his methodology. Gone are the days, or so they should be, when patients were given discarded computer paper on which to do their drawings and a box of old crayons. However impoverished a patient's productions, they will be enhanced by quality materials. If the art therapist invests generously in the basic equipment, the patient will respond to and be encouraged by the underlying message of genuine respect for the art productions. The therapist must understand the significance of the way different materials evoke particular emotional responses and have varied effects on personality types, on specific moods, and on different psychiatric disorders. "For a person who already has a limitation in physical or mental skills, it is essential not to create more barriers by improper selection of materials for art expression" (Nadeau, 1984, p. 64). Someone who is having trouble containing overwhelming emotions will likely feel enormously threatened by free-flowing, watery paints that bleed into one another, eliminating clear boundaries between the various colors. On the other hand, a patient hungry for a cathartic experience will feel frustrated with a small selection of colored pencils when what he needs is a large container of gouache and thick brushes with which to smear freely. In a similar way, the sensitive choice of a suitable format can make a difference to the success of a therapy session. Jake (see Chapter 2) chose a small format that enabled him to concentrate and produce a series of well-articulated drawings. This choice, based on some inherent wisdom, facilitated his creativity. And there was a lesson in it for me, too. Both the unusually small page size and the assistance he found in using a picture to copy came out of Jake's own desire. He found his own medicine, as it were—the small page functioning as a containing space that gave him confidence and helped reduce the anxiety of failure. In addition, the presence of the picture in front of Jake provided him with the safety of a map of sorts, a structure from which he could then wander off as he chose, elaborating on his own interpretation of what he was looking at. Jake spent many creative hours in my room filling his small pieces of paper with his abstract lines and shapes that were "copies" of boats, landscapes, and portraits. The referral picture functioned as a barrier between himself and the frightening emptiness of the blank page.

The following is a list of materials that should be available in the therapy room:

1. A supply of well-sharpened graphite pencils with soft lead such as 2B and 3B. The aged usually suffer from impaired vision and cannot relate to very thin and delicate lines produced with hard pencils. In order to achieve a stronger line, they would have to press down hard, and this is often impossible because of weakness in their hands. Working with pencils can be helpful for the first few sessions with patients who are inexperienced with art activities. It is also generally suited to extremely anxious patients—the repetitive graphite lines, the sense of control, and the predictability of one color, all tend to have a calming and unthreatening effect.

2. A selection of colored pencil crayons, oil pastels, and chalks. These are easier to control than liquid paints and are suitable for lower-functioning patients in that they don't demand much skill or mastery in order to achieve simple results. They eliminate the need for the control of paintbrushes or for intermediate stages such as cleaning the brush, dipping the brush in the paint, or making judgments about how much paint to take, all of which can be problematic for patients with coordination difficulties. Pencil crayons are particularly suited to the patient who is in need of control, such as someone with an obsessive/compulsive personality condition, who needs to create a sense of order. However, it is important to match page size with material; colored pencils work well on small formats, whereas on a larger format, the marks or images tend to get lost, overwhelmed by the large surrounding white space. Good-quality chalks have a wonderful, intense range of colors and do not require much pressure, but they can be messy. For lower-functioning patients this messiness threatens their experience of mastery. Whereas, for some, the use of chalks can be experienced as an easy way to blend colors and marks, it can be disheartening for others as the movements of their hand on the page ruins a strong, well-defined line.

3. Liquid paints such as gouache and watercolor are satisfying but require some skill, control, and judgment. If the budget permits, inexpensive acrylic colors can also be a stimulating addition for higher-functioning patients. Acrylic paint is thick, intense, and vibrant and does not lose its intensity when dry.

4. Paper of different size, quality, and color. Sometimes an inexpensive, thin paper will suffice for quick sketches and scribble work or pictures

done with oil pastels or pencil crayons. But when liquid paint is being used, the paper should be thick, sturdy, and capable of containing the layers of color that are often applied. The page is both a concrete and metaphorical container of the art productions, while the paint is the expression of a patient's inner world: his feelings, confusion, and desires. Hence it is important that the paper be strong enough and reliable enough to contain and support these expressions. Paper that falls to pieces, rips, and disintegrates as it comes into contact with the patient's "expression," increases a sense of danger, further unraveling a weakened ego structure.

5. A variety of sturdy, good-quality brushes. "The brush is a tool, an extension of the hand, and it can "provide unlimited variety in stroke, and in dabbing, pulling and swirling of color" (Nadeau, 1984, p. 67). The therapist must be sensitive enough to permit the patient to choose his own brush size, but for certain patients whose judgment is impaired, it is better to monitor the choice. A patient should not be left to struggle with a thick brush as he attempts to create a contour line, nor with a thin brush as he tries to fill in a large area defined by a contour line. Sometimes, the therapist has to dip the brush into the paint each time it needs to be replenished and hand it over to the patient.

6. Cardboard and construction paper are needed for sustaining activities such as collages with materials other than paper—sticks, shells, beads, wool, and so forth—as well as a base for clay sculptures.

7. Clay, plastecene, and modeling dough are basic materials for sculpting and creating three-dimensional works. Many patients are happier with the creation of objects, which feel more real to them than a two-dimensional representation on a page. The smearing, rolling, and pounding of clay can be very satisfying in itself, even if it doesn't result in a finished product, eliciting as it does more aggressive energies and legitimizing a certain emotional freedom. With lower-functioning groups, patients will be very happy to roll clay into balls, snake shapes, or circular forms.

8. Additional odds and ends—beads, stones, seeds, ceramic tiles, boxes, pipe cleaners, tooth picks, wool, and so forth—can be useful. A therapist is always collecting materials that can be added to a patient's works—stuck into clay objects or onto boards, structured to form a creature, or combined to make an abstract form. Having a selection of soft, "feminine" materials, such as fabric, wool, transparent colored papers, and cotton, as well as more "masculine" materials, such as nails, pins, pieces

of wood, electric wiring, and insulating tape is important too. These satisfy different needs in each patient, not necessarily defined by gender. In order to express aggression, frustration, or desire for control, it is quite possible that a female patient will seek out the harder, sharper materials which are typically viewed as being more "masculine." The same goes for a man who might seek expression for the traditionally gentler, more feminine, urges and needs.

9. A stock of magazines is useful for collage work. They can even provide a very calming activity for reluctant or anxious patients as they leaf through the journals, commenting and sometimes ripping out pictures without making additional creative use of them. These may stimulate memories and longings and thus can be the subject of discussions. There should also be a stock of pictures that have already been selected and cut out of journals by the therapist and stored in a large box, through which patients can sift for ideas or stimulation.

STRUCTURING THE SESSION

There are different ways of structuring therapy sessions, each of which should be suited to the needs of a particular patient, the arrangements of the facility, and the therapist's working style and therapeutic bias.

Individual Sessions

For higher-functioning patients, who retain a reserve of insight and capacity for self-reflection, individual meetings are sometimes recommended. Dementia is increasingly being diagnosed at earlier stages of onset, so that therapists will be seeing a growing number of patients who are aware that they are in a process of cognitive decline. This is an extremely anxious period, and the privacy of these individual sessions should be used to process related issues. Families are often ignorant about Alzheimer's or feel uncomfortable about revealing painful facts to their loved ones regarding the progressive nature of the disease. The therapist will judge how much information to give a particular patient, assess how much he is capable of absorbing, and attempt to present the reality. The therapist will also make space for the patient to express shock, denial, anger, or depression, thus helping him come to terms with his illness. These first, intimate meetings with the therapist can function as a bridging period as patients share their worries and acclimatize to the new environment of the geriatric unit. Therapists can help in the absorption process, provide an opportunity to ventilate concerns, and introduce suspicious and unsettled patients to the possibility of art activities that are available to them. Once a relationship is established with a familiar figure, patients are less likely to fear revealing themselves to other group members. Unfortunately, in most geriatric settings, the practical considerations of a large patient load and few therapists militates against the luxury of many individual sessions. But, where permitted, these can be shorter in duration (about half an hour), and in most cases no more than four to six sessions will be needed before the patient can join a group.

Open Workshops

In an open workshop, the therapist is stationed in the art room for several hours while the patients are free to come and go as they like, for as long as they like. Some preparation is required as the therapist recruits what she considers to be suitable candidates, by consulting with the staff and sitting and talking to patients during time that is unoccupied by other activities. In the art room, the therapist will not be shy to approach, persuade, and stimulate curiosity, all in the hope that the room will gradually become a place toward which patients will gravitate, finding there a source of pleasure, relaxation, and personal creativity. This only succeeds with high-functioning patients, who still have the capacity to initiate and to energetically choose activities that please them.

Group Sessions

My preference for the dementia patient is group work, where patients can be part of a community, an experience so lacking in their lives. Even when there is no real, logical conversation going on, a sense of togetherness can be read in the increasing pleasure expressed as the weeks go by.

Because dementia patients need a lot of individual attention, groups must be kept small. Five to twelve participants is appropriate, and if there are more than six, there should be an assistant for the art therapist. Left to their own devices, Alzheimer's patients often lose interest, forget the nature of the task, doze off, or stroll out of the room. Art therapy with this population demands an enormous amount of energy on the part of the therapist to compensate for the cognitive decline of the patients. The assistant must be attentive to those who are excessively confused, who have become too anxious, who have lost confidence in what they are doing, or who don't know how to go on after the first few marks. The group sessions do not involve group dynamics but, rather, provide a set up in which a number of people work on their own creative tasks within the security and energy of a small, safe group that is involved in similar activities. At its best, the session consists of two different mood states. The meeting is initially more social and outgoing, with patients greeting each other and negotiating their choice of seat. The therapist takes on a reassuring role, reminding participants about the previous week's work, talking about the plan of the present session, and generally providing patients with a means of warming up to the idea of artwork. However, once the work has begun, the room becomes quiet as participants become involved in more interior work, each contemplating his own page, grappling with his creative task. I discourage conversation during this part of the session, though usually the silence is a natural and integral response to the commencement of creativity.

Group sessions can be strictly structured in that from the outset there is a prescheduled time frame comprising an allocated number of sessions. A therapist must try to match an appropriate mix of patients the way one would any group-therapy session. No new patients are encouraged to join midway through a series. However, the reality of institutions for the aged makes it very difficult to maintain such a rigid program. Patients often drop out in the middle of a sequence of meetings and cannot be persuaded to rejoin the group. Raising issues of commitment and responsibility will not persuade the reluctant Alzheimer's patient to continue to participate. And though it is not recommended, the therapist often succumbs to staff pressure to include additional, problematic patients in the sessions. My solution has been to work toward a semistructured group, trying to retain a certain core group of regular participants but allowing for new members to be added at a pace that will not undermine the group process.

STRUCTURING A GROUP SESSION

The group sessions should be about one-and-a-half hours in duration and consist of three stages: the warm up, the art activity, and processing.

The Warm-Up

The warm-up is a term taken from the field of psychodrama, in which the challenge of the therapist is to lead the protagonist into the drama that lies ahead. The "cold group" tends to be unresponsive until it is "warmed up" (Jennings, 1986, p. 21), in much the same way that an athlete stretches and bends until his muscles are primed and he is ready to compete. The therapist must gain the interest of the group members and overcome their initial anxiety and reluctance to expose inadequacies, so that they become active, alert, engaged, and ready to take creative risks. She will use her inventiveness to distract the participants from the confusing outside world and assist them in connecting with their emotional, inner world by them turning art materials into marks, images, and colors on the page or into three-dimensional sculptures.

Many factors inhibit the commencement of an art activity. Organic brain damage often implodes on the natural ability to initiate. Patients many times feel shame and embarrassment for what they experience as their growing impairment, or, alternatively, they regard the use of art materials as an infantile activity that demeans them even further as they try to cling to their self-respect. In the higher-functioning groups, because of greater patient insight, shame and pride need to be overcome, and the therapist will seek ways to encourage and reassure the patients. In the lower-functioning groups, where cognitive and perceptual difficulties have taken a more profound hold, the problem of lethargy and lack of interest will dominate.

Various art-therapy texts describe warm-ups that are appropriate for Alzheimer's groups: *Art Therapy for Groups*, by Marian Liebman (1986); *Expressive Therapy with Elders and the Disabled*, by Jules Weiss (1984); and *The Art of Art Therapy*, by Judith Rubin (1984). The types of exercises chosen must constantly be referenced against patient capacities and against the rule of thumb that the aim is to energize rather than frustrate and to excite but not overwhelm. But ultimately it is personal experience that will help therapists choose activities to lead into artwork.

Physical exercise. Physical exercise is a very useful warm-up for Alzheimer's patients. The combination of tiredness, despair, additional illnesses, and medications results in participants who are very often physically lethargic and sleepy; their bones ache, their heads hurt, and their blood pressure is low. A short routine of simple movements such as clenching and unclenching fists, waving the hands in the air, and stamping on the ground raises the heart rate, gets the blood flowing, makes muscles more flexible, and helps get the body ready for action. There is the additional effect of giving the participants a sense of belonging to a group as they watch each other engage in a unified activity. Finally, and most importantly, the exercises can be fun, particularly if accompanied by music, making patients feel active, lively, and more optimistic.

Introductory discussions. Introductory discussion relating to a particular theme will help lead into the work. This can be elaborated through brainstorming, sharing stories, and writing participants' responses on a board. For example, if the therapist plans to initiate the drawing of portraits, it can be helpful to show some portraits done by familiar and famous artists. This increases a sense of a cultural milieu and provides confirmation of their existence as intelligent adults, allaying the often-expressed anxiety that they are being invited to engage in infantile activities. Many patients will come into the room, glance around at the cheerful colors, the sheets of paper, and the clay and ask derisively, "Do you think we are children?" Talking about Picasso's distorted portraits, Matisse's paper cutouts, and Dubuffet's primitive paintings will partly help them understand that regressive and "raw" art has a strong place in the creative world. It is worth sharing Picasso's famous declaration that it took him until age eighty to be able to draw like a child. Though it's unlikely this statement will be understood by many in its full depth, it does provide some justification for art that is simple and naive and is consoling for the patients who perceive themselves as unskilled and their work as unworthy. Other ideas for leading into portrait work can be tried: providing a mirror for each patient, so that they can spend time looking at their image; asking each patient to point out a noticeable feature of another member of the group; and presenting masks for inspiration. The therapist can instruct them to shut their eyes and touch and feel different parts of their own faces. Patients can be invited to pull certain faces—to smile, grimace, and scowl. These warm-ups connect them with their physicality and often raise the level of the drawing that follows. Such exercises give the group members a chance to engage in a nonverbal dialogue, enhance humor, and result in more invested creative activity.

Stimulating the senses. Since the language skills of dementia patients are diminishing, both in terms of understanding and articulation, it is helpful to stimulate as many of the other sense modalities as possible as compensation for the loss. Supposing the project is the creation of a collage of food images, preparatory work before it begins will widen the interest and the scope of the responses, providing the project with an emotional imperative rather than turning it into a mere technical task. Bringing in a few different food items for the group to taste could enliven the experience, as would talking about what they like to eat and what is healthy and what is unhealthy. They might want to smell items that have distinctive odors, such as mint, fish, onions, or garlic. Eliciting memories of their parents' cooking will stimulate other early memories.

Artifacts from the past. Items connected with the past that have not been seen for a long time—old tea sets, a black dial telephone, prewar sepia photos, an old radio, and so forth—will often wake up even the sleepiest member of the group. Alzheimer's patients live in a world that is becoming increasingly unrecognizable, not only because of perceptual and memory problems but because objectively it is a very different world from the one that they inhabited for significant parts of their lives. The memories of their childhood are taking more prominence as they lose the current ones, and in many ways such patients reside more in the past than in the present. Introducing a vintage object, one that releases undamaged long-term memory, brings up the old, familiar world and its connections to loving parents (at best), siblings, different climates, and former homes. Much liveliness and excitement often result from such an event, and when magazines are subsequently presented for collage work, there is likely to be far greater interest in the task, making it easier for the patient to choose pictures that really feel meaningful.

A variety of visual material. If the session is without a designated theme, it is important that there be a wide variety of visual material available to stimulate a desire to touch, experience, and investigate what is out there and accessible for them to "play" with—pictures to cut out, portraits to copy, colored shapes to stick on a page, and art books with reproductions from which to get ideas. Secondhand bookstores are a wonderful resource of inexpensive old art books containing colored reproductions. However, the amount of available material recommended will depend on the robustness of the particular participants. Very confused patients, who struggle to make sense of stimuli, will do much better when their choice is limited, sometimes to no more than three colors and a very small sheet of paper.

Music. Music can be used as a stimulus to creative activity. I usually choose two or three pieces with very distinct and different beats or rhythms—a tango, followed by a slow waltz, and finally a very rhythmic piece with strong percussion beat. Each of these should come as a contrast to the previous one. Participants are given paper and drawing material to hold in their hands before the music begins. I suggest they listen and move their hands on the page to the sounds they hear. With higher-functioning groups I suggest adding other colors or choosing another material, such as charcoal or oil pastels, when they want. When a group is very reticent, I take crayon and act as a role model displaying, in an exaggerated manner, a variety of optional movements. This helps them take more risks and expand their repertoire as they dare to lift their hands off the page, sway with the upper body, or thump hard with the crayon on the page.

The Art Activity

The therapist working with many other populations can stimulate an idea, provide an appropriate warm-up, and then sit back and watch the creative process take hold as patients work eagerly and use materials inventively. Such a satisfactory outcome would fit in with a guiding principal for facilitating authentic creativity, which is to be minimally directive, with choices allowed whenever possible to come from the patient rather than being imposed by the therapist.

Unfortunately, dementia patients often lapse into inertia and passivity and are quite likely to stare into space or even fall asleep if left to their own devices. A delicate balance between freedom and intervention is called for in order to accommodate the particular needs of such patients, and the therapist must accept the paradox that control and spontaneity, structure and freedom, rules and free expression all coexist, one having no meaning without the other. The blank page can be an intimidating space for an impaired person. He can easily be overwhelmed by projects that provide too much freedom or choice. Due to organic brain damage, his repertoire of pictorial language, imagination, and inner resource is often very limited. Ambiguity, instead of being an opening for creativity, can be a source of anxiety and cause the "artist" to withdraw. So, although any initiative that comes from the patients should be encouraged, Alzheimer's patients do need very close direction and guidance. For most, creativity will not occur without the structuring intervention of the therapist. The challenge is to be active, enthusiastic, involved, directive, and supportive without stifling remaining internal liveliness by encouraging compliance and dependence. Effort should be made to initiate activities that are likely to increase a sense of success and mastery and prevent exposure to failure and more frustration.

Because patients so easily lose track of an idea, uncomplicated exercises are preferable to projects that have multiple stages and continue from meeting to meeting. Instructions and explanations need to be simple, clear, and repeated often. The language of therapy that has become a common part of modern culture to discuss emotional development and personal growth is not familiar to many geriatric patients. Talking about one's feelings is likely to be frowned on in a population that grew up the first quarter of the twentieth century; therapy for many of them is for the insane; art, an activity for children. In addition, when first asked to pick up a crayon or pencil, there is often suspicion that they are being tested, as they were when being diagnosed with Alzheimer's.

A litmus test of a successful group art-therapy session is in the diversity of the final products, even when a specific project is given. The more diverse and varied the results, the greater the likelihood that there has been an internal process, and that the art production is colored in some way by the personal experience of each particular patient. The different representations of the same still life (Figures 3.1 and 3.2) reflect two different personalities, both of whom are struggling to contain their emotions, each in his own way. The pictures were drawn during a group session in which a vase filled with cherries was set

Figure 3.1. Cherries in a vase, 1.   **Figure 3.2. Cherries in a vase, 2.**

Two patients respond differently to the same still life, a reflection of their different internal experiences.

up as a still life. In Figure 3.1 the vase is tilted to the left with some of the haphazardly arranged cherries spilling out. In a totally different representation of the same still life (Figure 3.2) the contour of the vase is well-formed, providing a sturdy container for the meticulously arranged cherries inside. Each drawing can be read as metaphorical language that provides clues to the way in which the internal life molds what is perceived. The well-centered vase intimates control and balance (in spite of mild Alzheimer's symptoms) in a man who still feels able to organize his private world, keeping it safe from outside invasion. The vase in Figure 3.1 portrays emotional imbalance and a threat to this person's capacity to be master of his internal world.

When the final products in an art group are very similar, it is likely that the work has been technical and imitative rather than emotional and creative. More creative work is elicited when the therapist is careful not to become attached to a project as he had planned it. If patients go off on a complete tangent, with no regard for instructions, the therapist should take pleasure from the fact that they are working and involved. The project ceases to matter, since it is always preferable to elicit personal creativity rather than to encourage compliance with instructions.

The art therapist working with Alzheimer's patients must reconcile himself to the severe limitations of his patients and celebrate whatever they are still able to accomplish, relinquishing understandable wishes for greater displays of creativity; this may be a somewhat tall order for art therapists, many of whom are by their very nature creative and spontaneous people. The therapist must often be satisfied with even such minimal freedoms as the patient choosing his own color, voluntarily leaning over the table to take a page, or requesting a particular picture from a magazine to copy. In my experience, patients can repeat the same theme or project over and over and take pleasure in it every time. The picture is seldom a mechanical repetition of the previous one, but because of a limited repertoire, patients often return to the image that originally attracted them. Exposed as they are to such enormous changes as those their basic cognitive processes are undergoing, repetition might well function as a consolation, an experience of continuity and an exploration of the expected. Even in the art world this is not an unusual phenomenon: some artists have limited themes that they elaborate on throughout their lives, though obviously with greater skill and control of the material.

Increasingly, dementia patients find it hard to process what they see, touch, or hear. There are patients for whom the coordination of putting glue on the back of a picture and then sticking it on the page is too complex. The therapist must intervene before he feels frustrated, foolish, and defeated and provide instead material that the patient can control. As the disease progresses and the patient's internal world becomes more chaotic, it is important that the therapist sees to it that the sensations "are monitored and controlled to their benefit" (Khan-Denis, 1997, p. 197).

Over the years, I have found the following exercises to be useful. In most cases, with some adjustment, they can be applied to both low- and high-functioning patients and used in individual or group work.

Mandala drawings. In Mandala drawings, the circular form is used as the basic format for the art. Circles have been used throughout the ages as a symbol of wholeness, and Jung used them as a means of self-therapy during a prolonged period of emotional distress. For dementia patients, the stimulus of a circle drawn for them on a page, or the presentation of a page already precut into the form of a circle, provides a safe space, a prepared domain in which to begin their activity (Figure 3.3). The circle can provide "order and balance to one whose disordered thoughts, memories and feelings may be difficult or impossible to access" (Couch, 1997).

Landscapes. Landscapes present a simple and satisfying theme that can be repeated often and enjoyed by both lower and higher functioning patients. In the warm-up to the activity, participants can be shown how to form the basic divisions such as earth and sky, sky and ocean, mountains and ocean, using various hues of brown and blue. A predrawn horizontal line through the page proves to be an inviting and fairly simple stimulus for a landscape picture. This work can be prefaced with a theme, such as the issue of weather or the effect of seasonal change on trees, colors, moods, and emotions. The therapist can show paintings of very different landscapes such as deserts, forests, and Arctic scenes, pointing out the effects of change in colors.

Figure 3.3. Mandala. A scene of active village life contained within the safety of the circle.

Templates. For lower-functioning patients, or for those who simply cannot begin to use art materials without guidance, the provision of a "template or pattern of regressive images" (Harlan, 1990, p. 101), is a good means to initiate an artwork. The therapist prepares a set of images, either figurative or abstract shapes in contour form, which the patient fills in, elaborates on, or continues beyond its borders. Outlines of various containers—vases, pots, abstract shapes such as circles or squares, houses, various simple animal forms, trees, and contours of a head or an entire body—have proved useful. When provided with a prepared body outline, patients respond in quite idiosyncratic ways. Some attend to the background, introducing a partner (a longed-for companion?) or a house, showing concern for the people or the places to which they belong or from which they feel dislocated. Others are more interested in facial features or concern for body parts and clothing, indicating more interest in self-image (Figure 3.4).

Picture segments as a stimulus. After segments of abstract-art reproductions or pictures from magazines have been selected and glued to a page by the therapist, they are used as a focus, or starting point, for work. Portions of

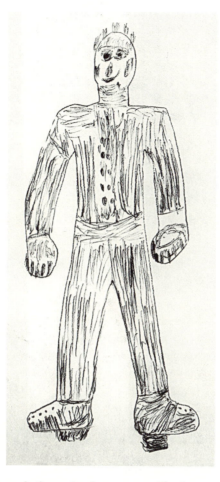

Figure 3.4. Completing a body contour. The figure stands alone, disconnected from the background, interacting with neither objects nor people.

bright abstract paintings, with clear colors and defined patterns, serve as an invitation to elaborate, extending existing shapes. Often, the artistic work has no visible connection with the fragment provided, yet one can observe the patient examining and visually responding to what is presented on the page. In a variation of this idea, each patient is given a page on which is glued a face or the head of a person taken from magazines. The patients are invited to create the rest of the body and to add items, such as a hat, a bag, or any other "gift." Sometimes more than one piece of abstract art is chosen, and the more skilled patient can combine the fragments with lines and colors (Figure 3.5).

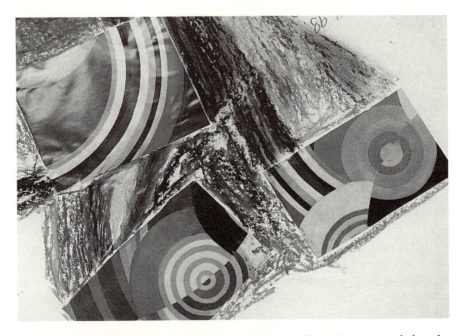

Figure 3.5. Responding to preglued fragments. The patient responded to the color and shapes of the three abstract pieces by connecting them to form a unified abstract work.

The rainbow. The rainbow is a simple image that can be a most satisfying way to begin working with gouache paints. This exercise allows for differences in individual abilities, and the results are usually very pleasing. Though the project has the advantage of simplicity, the opportunity for personal expression is not to be underestimated, as can be witnessed by the quite different approaches to the project by the participants. Patients use the page in their own unique manner, either hugging the margins or painting very small rainbows that get lost in the middle of a page or, in the case of those with more expressive courage, using their whole arm to spread the curving lines over the entire surface using thick paint and wide brushes. The more withheld or compulsive patient might use thin brushes to create cautious arches on a smaller format, refusing to use more than two or three colors. For higher-functioning patients, who are not threatened by the loss of control, one can wet the paper in advance and watch the paint as it slowly seeps into the water, with one color spreading into the other.

Varying the format. Offering different size paper, as well as introducing unusual formats can have a provocative effect, evoking renewed interest in working. Pages can be small, or very large, elongated, or cut into odd shapes such as ellipses, moon shapes and star shapes. For the higher functioning patient, altering the color of the page will stimulate and create a challenge, as they become interested in the effects of colors on a dark, as opposed to light background.

Drawing from a still life. Working from a simple still life can provide much pleasure for participants in the early stage of Alzheimer's (Plates 5 and 6). The still life should consist of three or four objects that have simple forms and contrasting colors. For instance, a vase with a flower or two in it is usually manageable, and interest can be added with a ceramic animal, bird, or figure placed on a piece of colored fabric. The patients who have less control or more perceptual difficulties may need help positioning the objects on the page, but care must be taken to only assist, not to take over the page and risk outshining the patient (Figures 3.6 and 3.7).

Figure 3.6. Still life, 1.   **Figure 3.7. Still life, 2.**

In Figure 3.6 the patient first used her artistic skills to complete the vase and flowers and as an afterthought provided a table that only barely manages to support the vase, which is precariously perched near the edge. In Figure 3.7 the patient used circular rows of color, achieving a work with an abstract quality.

Collage. Collages can be created using a variety of papers, such as tissue paper, old wallpaper, crepe paper, and so forth. The therapist can precut paper in various shapes and sizes from which the patient selects what he wants to use and glues it to the page. This is decorative work with little expressive value, but it is a fun activity and no small contribution to people with few sources of pleasure. It has the benefit of being easy and satisfying and providing pleasant results, beneficial either for beginners in an art group or for anxious and self-critical patients. Silver and gold paper often creates additional visual interest, as do papers with differing textures. Beads, stones, and dried flowers can be provided as a way to make the results livelier.

Joint artwork of therapist and patient. Sometimes, in order to have one-to-one contact with a patient, it is useful to work together on the same page. A simple, nonverbal conversation ensues as patient and therapist alternately make their marks and wait for the other to respond—what cannot be communicated through conversation is expressed in the subtle interaction of the art materials. Attention is paid to where the patient chooses—usually quite unconsciously—to place his mark, shape, or color. Through such choices he will be communicating a desire to distance himself from the therapist, a need for intimacy and closeness, or, by smearing over the therapist's lines, unexpressed aggression or competitiveness. This same dialogue can be attempted with more timid patients, using subdued watercolors or colored crayons. It can also be done with clay, which the therapist and patient use to make shapes and combine them into a collaborative sculpture. Another of the many possibilities is a pleasant encounter in which therapist and patient draw an outline of their hands on the same page, which they then color or decorate.

Portraits/masks on predrawn outlines of a head. A collection of photo-copied outlines of heads for use as the basis for portraits is worth having in one's supply of materials. Patients are invited to fill in facial features and to add clothing or other elements to the background (Plates 7 and 8). A dialogue bubble can be drawn as an invitation to the patient to fill in some words that the mask or portrait is saying. This becomes an opportunity for patients to explore and articulate uncomfortable feelings they are not consciously aware of or are reluctant to acknowledge, such as loneliness, shame, and anger. The few words can provide information about the emotional state of the patient and be used as a basis for the therapist to reflect back and verbally articulate patients' concerns in a way that they are incapable of doing.

For higher-functioning patients the instructions can be more elaborate. For instance, the participant is invited to create two masks—one happy and one sad, one angry and one loving, and so forth—and then each mask is asked to say something about himself, giving the patient an opportunity to express conflicting internal voices (Figure 3.8). Patients enjoy copying portraits from art reproductions that should be made available to them (Plates 9, 10, 11, and 12).

The mother/child image. Over the years, I have collected images of the mother/child couple. Patients often feel themselves to be dependent and needy and in many cases talk of their parents as though they were still alive. This would explain why these pictures are of such great interest to them and why they stimulate conversations in the group about this idealized relationship. When it comes to trying to copy any of these pictures, the results are usually unimpressive and confused because it takes much skill to draw two figures entangled with each other, even for the most skilled of artists. But the emotional impulse has the power to drive them on with concentration and apparent satisfaction.

Providing pictures to copy. Providing patients with pictures to copy is a means to initiate art activity. I have seen patients earnestly and repeatedly referring to the picture they had selected, glowing with satisfaction at the image they have produced, even though it bears little similarity to the original. Somehow the presence of the picture provided structure, filled the sometimes-daunting empty white page, and gave them a starting point for their own work. It might

Figure 3.8. Two masks on prepared contours. In these two masks drawn by the same mute patient, the mouth is noticeably absent. This could be a reflection of the increasing loss of the use of language and the frustration that inevitably follows.

only be one line or color that they manage to copy, but if the picture engages them, they will struggle to take a part of it for themselves. In Plate 13, Henry Moore's sculpture was the inspiration for the colorful rendition of the lounging woman. Figure 3.9 contains recognizable elements of a Miró painting.

Taking into consideration a patient's poor eyesight and often confused perception, therapists should provide a choice of pictures that are bold and clear

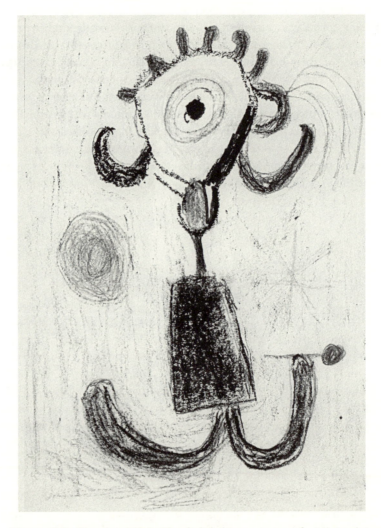

Figure 3.9. Copying Miró. The slightly bizarre image of a Miró painting attracted this patient who used whichever elements pleased her own surrealistic image.

and that as much as possible have distinct boundaries between one area of color and another. A still life with a vase and a few flowers will be a manageable image, as opposed to one with a profusion of small, many-colored flowers in an elaborately designed vase.

Drawing a tree. The tree exercise can be prefaced by reminiscing, recalling images of memorable trees in each person's life. Photographs or artists' portrayals of trees can spark interest, and photocopied outlines of trees in different shapes and sizes can be used for low-functioning patients to complete.

In the two renderings of trees by two different artist/patients, each has a quite distinct emotional impact, and reflects different personal responses to the theme. For instance, in Figure 3.10, the artist/patient has introduced an element of relationship into the project. An animal eats from the tree, bringing up issues of nurturing and generosity but also of possible aggression as the animal tears off pieces of the branch. These thoughts can be reflected to the patient in a gentle and accepting form in order to open a dialogue about current feelings. The tree in Figure 3.11, in sharp contrast, stands in the center of the page on a spindly trunk that is not rooted in the ground but emerges from the bottom of the page and has no contact with its surroundings. It resonates with

Figure 3.10. Tree, 1.   **Figure 3.11. Tree, 2.**

The picture in Figure 3.10 portrays a relationship of sorts, between the tree and the animal, as opposed to the solitariness of the tree in Figure 3.11.

loneliness, a response that the therapist might share with the patient in order to open up the issues of isolation or abandonment.

Working within a frame. A helpful method of providing the safety that is so cardinal in initiating creativity is to offer the patient a frame to work within. Pages of differing sizes with a variety of frames drawn in advance are photocopied and kept on hand. These help the patient cope with confused perception of boundaries, difficulties in perceiving inside and outside, of personal space as opposed to a neighbor's space. The frame acts as an extra boundary to that of the edge of the page, inside of which it feels safer to put one's marks (Figure 3.12). The patient might begin to use the frame to contain his image, but when the dementia is more advanced, it becomes difficult to remain within the boundaried space (Figure 3.13). Another way to create a "framing" experience is by providing a folder for each participant in which his work is stored and to which he has access. Though patients seldom remember the existence of this folder, the very ritual of opening it each week, seeing their name

 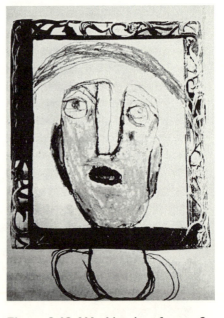

Figure 3.12. Working in a frame, 1.   **Figure 3.13. Working in a frame, 2.**

In Figure 3.12, the well-constructed head fits comfortably within the frame, indicating that emotional and cognitive functioning is reasonably intact. In Figure 3.13, the patient extends his drawing outside the framed area—a sign of greater cognitive deterioration.

written on it, removing the work, and then returning it to the file, all increase the security and predictability of the art-therapy room.

Modeling with clay. The opportunity to play with clay, to mold and form it, can be a relaxing and calming activity, although those with arthritic fingers may find it painful and initially want to avoid it. But if encouraged to touch the material in any way they can, they often enjoy it immensely, and there is an added benefit to underused joints. While some may initially reject working with clay, because of its messiness, it can ultimately provide much pleasure. Small balls of clay should be prepared on a board in front of each patient, who will be shown by the therapist how to roll, pound, smooth, hollow out, and cut the clay. Many patients spend time in the simple act of repeatedly rolling balls and snake-like forms, joining them together and breaking them up. Those with more ability will be delighted with any containing form that they can create, such as a vase or a pot, in which they can insert clay representations of fruit or other food. The higher-level patients will be able to mold simple human or animal forms and later dialogue with these forms, through which they communicate their desires and feeling. "If the aim of psychotherapy is getting in touch with the instincts, an engagement with clay is often . . . the most direct way," says Martina Thomson (p. 86), while for Margaret F. Keyes (1983), clay is a useful way to explore "sticky, messy, bad feelings" (p. 5).

Processing

Processing, the manner in which the art therapist deals with the finished product of patients, is always an issue of concern and dialogue. Marie Blank finds that, in general, a "more active inquiring role is required of the therapist working with the aged individual than with the younger persons" (Crosson, 1976, p. 56). Passivity, lower energy, and poor memory make it more difficult for them to track the phases of the process and less able to share thoughts about their art. Much depends on the therapist's delicate response, which can deepen the relationship and enhance trust, both of which are basic ingredients for the courage to create. This is a very significant part of the session, one that will affect the mood in which the patient leaves the room and will influence his desire to return. The therapist's task is to relate to the work that has been done, essentially communicating that he has witnessed it, accepted it, and appreciated it. Mirroring and demonstrating an active presence are great gifts that the therapist can give the increasingly marginalized patient.

The way a therapist chooses to respond to a patient's work depends to a large extent on the stage of the illness. One might well ask why a person who is cognitively impaired and who has never painted before would desire to pick up a crayon to make a mark. He risks making a fool of himself, believes it's a child's activity, and sees only a blank page in front of him, having no idea what to put on it. It is the therapist's task to make him want to take that step, and it is the way the therapist responds to his work that will have a cumulative effect in impelling him to "play" with art materials. Every visit to the art room should deepen the relationship with the therapist, making the patient feel safer and giving him confidence that his work will be welcomed with kindness and respect.

The therapist will try to make sense of the symbolic communication of each work. It is on the basis of such understanding that he can facilitate the next project, directing the patient to materials and projects that are appropriate to his artistic intentions and his emotional explorations. The therapist will provide a verbal response to the image, always keeping in mind that the reading of the symbol is tentative. If he perceives disapproval or disagreement in the patient, he will honor those inclinations and resist imposing his vision. His response will not be an interpretation but an intuitive, empathic response, a mirroring or reflection based on his personal internal resonance with the art product. His task is to seek what seems to be the subtext of the work, the hidden narrative, and relate to that.

Morris, for example, almost exclusively drew pictures in which a tree was the central image. Talking of the tree, and not of Morris himself, I would wonder about how it felt to be so alone, and when he drew two trees, I would comment on the pleasure of being in the company of another. Sometimes I would generalize and reflect on the human condition, on our loneliness, our desire for closeness and warmth. On one occasion, using gouache paint, he fashioned a group of trees with a limited palette of blacks, browns, and grays. In the center he drew what at first looked like another small tree, to which he began to add orange and red. At the end of the session, I pointed out these warm colors, wondering what they were doing in this rather cold atmosphere. "It's a fire," he told me. I commented on the potential pleasure of such warmth, which brought him to childhood memories of his native town in Europe and of occasions when his family would gather around the fire. This led to a brief, but "warm" conversation in which Morris was clearly nostalgically connected with his childhood. The picture became "warmed" in an organic manner through the introduction of the orange and red color Morris had added, and it was now becoming even more alive through my verbal response to it and the "warm" memories it was bringing up. Such brief encounters when processing the artwork have much to do with transforming the art activity into a more profound experience; the patient speaks in metaphorical language, and the therapist reflects it by making sense of the symbols, articulating its possible emotional meaning, and saying the words that he cannot.

Because the Alzheimer's patient is emotionally quite regressed and defense-less, it is not advisable to attempt any direct interpretation of the artwork in terms of revealed unconscious content. Any such revelations of profound, hidden personal issues are usually incomprehensible at best and likely to be point-lessly painful at worst. There is very little use that can be made of such information by the fragile, vulnerable, and forgetful people who will come to the art room. If one has become acquainted with the emotional issues being expressed, one can relate to them indirectly, through the art, without reference to the patient himself, thus touching on emotional meanings without under-mining fragile defenses.

Alzheimer's patients take a long time to process information and to find a response to an outside initiative. One cannot naturally assume from their si-lence that one has not been understood or that the patient is reluctant to enter into a dialogue. The relatively young and energetic therapist often errs when she concludes disinterest and leaves the aged patient behind as she hurries to solve other problems.

Zara (see Chapter 1) never came to the art room voluntarily, always needing to be coaxed and persuaded, and though it often appeared as though I could not get through to her, I learned to wait patiently, trusting that during the long si-lence, she would arrive at an internal decision to join the group. She repeatedly copied faces of babies, painstakingly working at the eyes, which always looked fragile and vulnerable. When she was given adult pictures to copy, these, too, very soon became the faces of helpless babes. I remarked on this emotional as-pect of her pictures, adding from time to time that we often long for the days when we were babies and were well taken care of. I would focus on the content of the picture such as the absence of any comforting figure for the baby. Expanding on this if I felt she was still concentrating, I would add that it is often quite scary to feel that we need to be taken care of, given that we are not sure that there are people we can trust. In this way, I hoped to resonate with her dependency long-ings that she conveyed through her art, without shaming her by unnecessarily exposing what I guessed might be her need for mothering from me.

When processing the artwork within the group, various tasks can be given so that each participant can take an active role rather than remaining a passive viewer. For instance, each person can think of a name for any particular work, which the therapist can then write on a page and, after the list is compiled, read out to the whole group. The creator himself could be given the choice of dis-carding certain words not relevant to his picture, leaving only the words or sen-tences that appeal to him. It is another way of extending the experience of being attended to, of being central and thus of boosting self-worth. This is only appro-priate in high-functioning groups, demanding concentration and an ability for abstraction. An example of such work can be seen in the powerful poetic responses contributed by participants after they drew pictures related to the mother/child theme (see Chapter 2).

Information regarding premorbid personality (i.e., before the onset of the illness) can be helpful in making sense of the symbolic meaning of visual distortions in the artwork. Experience and intuition will be called for in order to distinguish which of the distortions, reductions, and perseverations are due inherently to pathological brain function and which reflect the personal patterns of the patient.

There is generally a large age gap between the Alzheimer's patient and the therapist. If the therapist is in her twenties or early thirties, there might be a difference of three generations. A therapist who grew up in the 1970s relating to a patient who was a child early in the twentieth century must recognize the accompanying differences in values, language, and experiences. Research shows that older adults learn word lists better when the lists are made of older words as opposed to more current language, which indicates that "word usage changes over time and suggests that therapists need to consider using appropriate word choices when communicating with older adults" (Knight, 1992, p. xiii). In order to understand the "other," one must have some knowledge about their cultural background, values, childhood and adult experiences.

An elderly man, in one of the meetings that revolved around the subject of eating habits and favorite foods, chose to draw something that I could not recognize but transpired to be a locust. He shyly explained that during World War II there was a shortage of food, and the children would set out pots to catch the locusts and cook them. "They were delicious," he enthused. "I can still remember the crackly sound they made when we opened up the shells." The slight revulsion I felt made me realize how different was the world in which this man grew up; it was a world of deprivation, uncertainty, and hunger, in which he needed to nourish himself in any way he could. These were the early memories that were still somehow etched in his mind and to which I needed to connect, erasing my own mental images of sweetly dressed babies in nurseries with pastel-colored furnishings. The more one avails oneself of knowledge about the past to which patients belong, the more one can find a language with which to communicate with them and understand the themes being expressed in their art. One's very curiosity about a patient's past, and desire to learn how life was for them—which may be very different from one's own experiences—will enhance the relationship.

In every therapeutic choice, from the nature of the exercises to verbal interventions, the central message of the room should prevail and be communicated in as many subtle ways as possible: that this is a room of freedom and creativity, that one need no artistic skill in order to enjoy the activity, that there are sources of help and guidance if they have trouble making decisions, and that involvement with art materials is encouraged, but their need to take their time will be respected. I do not refer to the art as therapy, but rather talk of art as an alternate language, one that can be used to express many different feelings and moods, even negative ones. This should not be turned into a long lecture, because attention span is short and most of what is said will quickly be forgotten. It is the therapist who must hold this intention within and constantly communicate it in both concrete and symbolic ways. The therapist's constant attention to patients' creations, regardless of the quality, will communicate a deep sense of respect for the artistic product. Above all, the therapist's role is to constantly encourage, support, and accept but never to criticize. Needless to say, there are occasional impressive artistic products that will be of great satisfaction both to the therapist and to the patient, but this is an auxiliary compensation. The quality of the artwork is not the aim of the session; rather, it is the facilitation of participants' vital investment in working with the materials and in so doing giving life to a world that is becoming more and more dormant.

While working on his creation, the artist/patient is hopefully fully engaged in an internal process. At best—and this is not always the case at all—he is silent, caught up in some struggle with making marks on a page or modeling a piece of clay, subtly supported by the other quiet participants sitting around the art table. In the hushed privacy of the intimate group, an internal experience is spurring him on to continue refining, adding, or changing. This is the time for silent, contemplative work, motivated by a personal need and not by the desire to please or achieve. Finally, when the work is done and he feels he has no more to add, or the hour is up, the session will come to an end. The creative period is over, the silence is broken, some words may be exchanged about the making of the work, and the participant will leave the room to face the large, open spaces, the noise, and, perhaps ironically, the isolation of the anonymous public area. Achieving closure by using simple recurring rituals, such as repeated words of farewell, that provide predictability and continuity serves as an important bridge between these two very different experiences, ending what has been and hopefully making it a bit easier for the patients to take part in the group when next it meets.

4

✳

THEORETICAL PERSPECTIVES

"I could draw it" a dreamer often says to us, "but I don't know how to say it."

—*Sigmund Freud*

Art therapy, the use of art materials for the making of marks and images within the context of a therapeutic relationship, brings together two complementary disciplines and combines them into a new and separate endeavor. This chapter shows how pictorial image making began to be used for psychotherapeutic purposes and how it proved to be a valuable therapeutic enterprise that is slowly being adapted for work with Alzheimer's patients. While anecdotal evidence and case histories provide a lively picture of the way in which art therapy affects the world of dementia patients, it is also important to examine the theoretical and conceptual basis for the work. There is always interplay between theory and practice, so that one's intuitive clinical interventions gain credibility when they are based on sound theoretical principles. When it comes to articulating the rationale for one's assumptions, one needs to show not only how art therapy works but also why it works.

Expressive therapy is a global term for any of the therapies that use a host of different expressive media as the central tool of healing. Each of them proposes an expressive means of communication as an alternative or addition to verbal language. Part of the interest in these expressive modes came about as a response to dissatisfaction with purely verbal therapies. It was felt that though they often provided an extended vocabulary for the patient to describe his suffering, often they led to no real changes. In addition, there are many patients whose specific mental or emotional limitations preclude the use of a purely

talk-based therapy. The introduction of the creative media was seen to introduce a new dimension into the therapeutic encounter. Primarily it could be
seen to bypass the restrictions of the logical, conscious mind, which operates
through intellectual understanding, and access unspoken internal forces. Early
in the twentieth century, Jung, considered by many to be the father of art therapy, expressed his belief in the power of painting, displaying a deep respect for
the unconscious (the source of creativity), not as a receptacle for pathological,
repressed material (as did Freud), but for its power to heal. His interest in creative work grew out of his teachings on Active Imagination, in which he encouraged engagement with materials like paint, clay, or sand or in an activity
such as dance or music making. Essentially the person was encouraged to let
things happen, allowing the material to be shaped without conscious intention. Throughout his life, Jung drew, painted, and sculpted, particularly when
he was undergoing personal stress, and he encouraged his patients similarly to
make visual representations of their dreams and fantasy material. According to
Bernie Warren (1984), artistic creation has been isolated from the general
population in many ways, defined as the responsibility of the few gifted individuals and relegated to museums walls. In such a way, the mass of society has
been denied their right as human beings to the spontaneous act of creativity.
The reintroduction of the arts as a wider endeavor answers a universal need
for each and everyone of us to "reaffirm ourselves and to communicate with
others" (p. 3).

Various prominent theoreticians view the advantages of art therapy in different ways. For Harriet Wadeson (1980) its power lies in the compelling nature of "shared meaning," and of communication. It enables the concrete
creation of a "personal vision that through transformation into an art object
may be shared with others" (p. 4). Edith Kramer (1971) emphasizes the inte-
grative and healing property of the creative process itself, a process that does
not require the addition of verbal reflection. The simple involvement in the
creative act itself is the therapy.

The use of art as a means of healing was evidenced long before an official
profession was declared, making it hard to pinpoint the exact beginnings of art
therapy as a distinct discipline. References to art and its healing properties are
a universal, age-old phenomenon. As early as biblical times, mention was
made of the power of David to soothe the tormented soul of King Saul by playing the harp. Many traditional artists, while not relating to art as a therapy,
have acknowledged that it has played an essential role in their emotional survival. Hans Prinzhorn, a philosopher and later a psychiatrist, collected the art-
works of mental patients in 1921, valuing them as profound expressions of the
psyche and as manifestations of a primal creative urge that belongs to all

human beings. In 1938, Adrian Hill after a lengthy hospitalisation due to TB coined the term "art therapy," by which he meant simply that the art does therapeutic work. He was referring to the way he used drawing quite unwittingly, during his protracted recovery period. So happy was he with the effects of this on his emotional well-being that he urged others to paint—not to copy, but to express what they were feeling at the time of the painting. Others regarded their belief in creativity as a fundamental aspect of aliveness. Rollo May (1975) talked of creativity as "a necessary sequel to being" (p. viii), and he was fascinated and excited at the simple act of watching two colors merge into an unpredictable third. Roberta Nadeau wrote, rather poetically, that the "wonderful beauty of the arts . . . is the fact of human emotion being involved in a raw and uncensored experience" (1984, p. 61). According to Tessa Dalley (1984), art and creativity are "an indigenous feature of every society," with "unique, universal, and ubiquitous properties for . . . application in therapy" (p. xii).

Margaret Naumberg pioneered the fairly new discipline of art therapy in the 1940s, and over the years it gradually became part of medical institutions, hospitals, and education systems, as well as being used in private therapeutic settings. It has been applied to and modified for a wide range of problems, such as psychiatric illness, mental retardation, autism, and delinquency. Various explanations of the therapeutic agent of these art activities continue to be offered, depending on the therapist's educational background and theoretical leanings and on the particular population being addressed. In her book *Approaches to Art Therapy,* Judith Rubin (1987) brings together these theoretical approaches to art therapy and shows how they are translated into the clinical work. There is, however, one fundamental belief that is common to all these uses. Whereas for the artist the prime motivation of the art activity is the end product, when it is co-opted into therapy it is the process that is central; in the latter, art activity becomes an alternative means of expression and communication, which can in certain situations be the catalyst for emotional and behavioral changes.

Over the years it became important to distinguish between the activities promoted in the occupational-therapy setting as opposed to the creative work encouraged in art therapy. Observed from the outside, a group of patients who are cutting and gluing colored paper could as easily be involved in an occupational-therapy group as an art-therapy group. There is, however, a vast difference. Oliver Sacks (1985) illuminated this difference when he described the art of an autistic artist who "seemed to have clear powers of imagination and creativity." When this man copied an illustration of a canoeing scene on a lake from a magazine, it "was not *a* canoe, but *his* canoe that emerged in the drawing" (p. 207). This is the essence of the really creative act: the product is not judged on its artistic merit, success, or value as a piece of art, but is apprehended in terms of it being specific to a person, energized by his own unique history, experience, senses, and emotions. Decoration is not the aim, nor is keeping the person busy or using remaining skills. Though all of these are additional, desired by-products of the art therapy, they are not the central aim, which is to involve patients in a moment of true creativity. Of course, creative acts might occur in an occupational-therapy setting, but it is in art therapy that the focus is on helping the patient to create marks, lines, colors, signs, and symbols that are his own. Whereas the occupational therapist sets up activities with the aim of maintaining and restoring function and independence, the art therapist focuses on emotional expression and the facilitation of creative processes. As Sacks says of his autistic patient, maybe it was "not great art . . . perhaps it was child-art; but without doubt it was art of a sort" (p. 208). Not of *a* patient, but of *the* patient.

ALZHEIMER'S AND ART THERAPY

The central feature of art therapy, which gives it such natural potential as a healing agent for the condition of Alzheimer's, is the fact that it bypasses the need for verbal communication. Naumberg (1966) describes it thus: "Objectified picturizations act . . . as an immediate symbolic communication which frequently circumvents the difficulties of speech." Because of the language impairment in so many Alzheimer's sufferers, art activity is a particularly attractive therapeutic alternative. Taking into account the mounting difficulties encountered by the patient, it would not seem possible that he could be creative in the sense of bringing something new into the world, making new combinations, or making personal choices. Yet even the most apathetic patients, often unheard and discarded in facilities, units, hospitals, institutions, given the appropriate guidance and direction, will often produce works of surprising beauty (Rubin, 1987).

This experience with creativity has a visibly positive effect on patients whose opportunities to make any personal choices have been almost entirely eliminated. This is not only because of their diminished cognitive abilities but because in a busy, materialistic, competitive world, few people have the time or patience to match themselves to the slow pace of the person with dementia. Thus he is defeated doubly: internally by the disease that limits his capacities and slows him down and externally by an understandably impatient society that is more efficient than he is. He is slowly deprived of the opportunity to use even his surviving faculties, and a vicious cycle is set up. No more relied upon by others, the patient gradually withdraws into even greater passivity; given less responsibility, he is less willing to initiate, others take over, and he is rendered even more inactive. The involvement in any creative act is actually an opportunity for returning some responsibility to the patient, a reestablishment of faith in his abilities. The tendency to give up, to resort to helplessness, and to feel angry at disabilities is common in the Alzheimer's patient, who has less opportunity or will to struggle with difficulties, his capacity to bear frustration seriously impaired. It creates a problem for the therapist who, on the one hand, will try and protect the patient from giving up prematurely, and on the other, will want to present him with challenges that will extend his energies. Wherever possible, and this is a thin line that he walks, the therapist will refuse to make decisions for the patient and refuse to solve graphic dilemmas. He will present the patient with the burden of choices with which he will be encouraged to struggle, all the while trying to avoid the danger of discouraging him to the point of despair or surrender.

Annette Shore (1997), in her excellent article "Promoting Wisdom," examines the place of the struggle inherent in the creative art process. She believes that the failure to grapple with pain can result in a disconnected and dormant state and that there is no way around this struggle if one is to grow. It is up to the therapist working with low-functioning individuals, to structure, adapt to, and compensate for the client's disabilities, without attempting through overzealous interventions, to bring about easy resolution of the art experience. In fact, she warns, by so doing they may be preventing the very battle with the art materials and with their own resistance that can bring about the healing results. Shore presents a model that has implications for art therapy with the impaired geriatric population and shows how the successful resolution of developmental struggles through life results in particular adult capacities or limitations. These are expressed in the art productions, and even though they are impaired in form and lacking sophistication, the sensitive therapist can decipher them. The successful resolution of any struggle demands the use of ego strength, vital involvement, and enlistment of mature defense mechanisms in order to master previously raw affect. Though the gains may be particularly small and have only temporary effect, it is up to the therapist to come to terms with the value of providing such meaningful experiences in people whose life is slipping almost entirely into despair, inactivity, and passivity. While the cognitive impairment impedes organization of the process into conscious thoughts, the picture making enables, through displacement, the expression of powerful emotional statements. However, this process achieves its true richness through the tolerance for frustration and for the expressions of despair. If the therapist has the ability to contain and bear that struggle, she will give some courage to the patient, who then might use it in her own work. "Perhaps more important than any actual intervention is the art therapist's belief that active creative struggle can lead to personality reorganization. If the therapist conveys this belief through patience, acceptance and gentle prodding . . . the patient can internalize this belief" (Shore, 1997, p. 177).

ANCHORING ART THERAPY IN TRADITIONAL PSYCHODYNAMIC THEORY

Art therapy takes its impulse from two worlds, the belief in the power of the creative act itself as a life-affirming and sustaining activity on the one hand, and, on the other, respect and value for psychological theory and practice, which provide guidance and direction to the understanding of therapeutic processes. A complex relationship exists between these two disciplines, which once might have been considered conflicting but today are recognized as complementary. Though they differ with regard to many basic issues, such as the use of language in therapy, the importance of interpretations, and the value of transference relationships, it is possible for them to interact, nurture, and enrich each other.

Modern psychodynamic theories can help us understand some of the therapeutic processes that occur in art therapy involving Alzheimer's patients. However, most theories or systems depend on the patient having sufficient memory to connect disparate events and communications, a capacity for insight and self reflection, and an ability to transpose what is learned and absorbed in the therapy, whether consciously or unconsciously, beyond the therapy session. This might seem to exclude the notion of psychological therapy for Alzheimer's patients, who have diminished memory, tentative capacity for self-reflection, and a weakened defense system that would proscribe invasive interpretations. But a strong case can be made for an attenuated version of the therapeutic power of art therapy for Alzheimer's, in spite of these and other limitations. Because very little memory is available for the patient to make connections from one meeting to the next, each session must be regarded as a separate and whole experience, a here-and-now event that is expressed in the art. The one connecting, sustained factor is the consistent relationship with the therapist. Unfortunately, though, whatever gains are being made in the therapy have very short-lived effects, because of the ongoing destructive impact of the disease that will further impair the patient's cognitive abilities.

IMPORTANCE OF STRUCTURE

The creative act makes a connection between two seemingly conflicting modes of functioning. Creativity is energized by and accessed through chaotic, unconscious, regressive experiences, yet in order for this energy to be harnessed into a form and a structure, a different aspect of the psyche must be activated: the capacity for mastery and control. This ability to give external, concrete form to the internal, amorphous matter is empowering and no less important to healthy functioning than the ability to make contact with archaic, regressive, unconscious material. It is a startling achievement for the Alzheimer patient who is given a page on one side, and a box of crayons or some tubs of paint on the other to succeed in creating something new, something out of nothing—what Arieti (1976) calls a "Magic Synthesis." The Alzheimer's patient is particularly in need of the outward form, order, and structure. From experience, we know that he responds very badly to disorganization, to changes, and to the unpredictable. Faced with the crumbling structures of his mind, threatened by the inner sense of chaos, he needs a containing frame. This is provided concretely by the edges of the picture that define the limits of a territory or by contour forms prepared in advance. Within this framed space and within and around these contours, he can spontaneously add his marks, organizing the material paradoxically, through his free creative choices. Form and structure are essential for the spontaneous act, which would vanish into chaos without them. A scream cannot be a poem until the pain or joy that energizes it is molded and structured into a concrete expressive mode. Clearly the mental deterioration caused by dementia has an impact on the quality of any art product, but it does not preclude transformation of drives into structured forms. However, a certain amount of clarity is the necessary condition for taking the risk of making marks on what is experienced as the empty and often threatening interior of a page. Rollo May (1975) describes the behavior of psychotic patients in hospitals who walk close to the walls: "They keep oriented to the edges, always preserving their localization in the external environment. Having no localization inwardly, they find it especially important to retain whatever outward localization is available" (p. 145). Those people blessed with a fairly well-structured and grounded sense of self have the capacity to tolerate chaos, disorganization, and lack of control. For such personalities, that which is vague and ill-defined can be fertile ground for creativity and adventurousness. But for the person who inhabits a more fragile world, it will only create anxiety and withdrawal. This is the fine balance that has to be struck between the two extremes of freedom and structure—assisting those patients living in an internally fractured world to enjoy and make use of the freedom in such a way that they will be protected from an open and limitless experience that could be experienced as highly dangerous.

THE CONCRETE FORM

The final artwork, the picture or sculpture, is a concrete form that comes out of the unconscious. Joy Schaverien (1992) describes it thus: "When a picture is made in therapy it may 'uncloak' an image of which the artist was previously unconscious. Once such an image is pictured it is 'out there' rather than internal, it can be seen and this effects a change from an unconscious state, in the artist, to a more conscious one. As a result of this, even without verbal interpretation, a transformation begins to take place in the inner world of the artist" (p. 7). With Alzheimer's patients, one could think of the effect of the image once created, as the effect of the fairy tale on the small child. The contents do not lead to a conscious understanding of the deeper meanings of the tale, yet they resonate with the profound currently felt emotions of the child and are understood in an internal and unarticulated manner. In the case of active creation of artwork, as opposed to the passive listening to a story recounted by another, there is the additional advantage of personal manipulation and energetic investment; the struggle with the material; the necessity, no matter how minimal, of making choices and mustering the energy to organize the images. For Schaverien, these powerful forces of creativity are the "world of the life of the nights . . . [which] thus becomes present in the midst of the life of the day" (p. 41).

FUNCTION OF THE ART THERAPIST

In many ways, "the art therapist functions as an artist and educator who is capable of modifying his working methods according to the patient's pathology and needs" (Kramer, 1971, p. 25). The therapist of the Alzheimer's patient must be familiar with art materials and ways to maximize the successful use of them. He is constantly trying to understand the emotional communications of his patients and to provide the appropriate responses to his world. He will avoid interpreting images back to patients, which would risk exposing them, in their vulnerable states, to overwhelming emotions or simply incomprehensible associations. Instead, he will use his knowledge to help his patients, within his limited abilities, to produce artwork that contains and expresses emotionally loaded material. Whatever art is done in art therapy sessions, all the painting, scribbling, scratching, sticking, and sculpting that happens will be viewed within the context of a relationship, and the therapist will examine the meanings of the relationship issues between himself and the patient that emerge as the art process is taking place. What the therapist can give the patient is supportive mirroring, providing a space and a means with which to give voice to the unconscious or the inexpressible. The purpose of the mirroring is to communicate to him that he has been understood; to translate into language, and therefore clarify for him, what he is feeling; to legitimize and universalize his feelings; and finally, and no less important, to respect his privacy and need for defenses by not exposing him to overwhelming internal material.

Tom Kitwood (1997) presents a provisional list of seven different types of positive interactions with Alzheimer's patients:

1. Recognition (acknowledgement as a person with a name and a history)
2. Negotiation (consulting about preferences, desires, and needs)
3. Collaboration (alignment in a shared task)
4. Timalation (forms of interaction in which the prime modality is sensuous, without the intervention of concepts and intellectual understanding, such as aromatherapy or massage)
5. Celebration (providing an ambience which is convivial, joyful, and expansive)
6. Relaxation
7. Play

There are three additional psychotherapeutic interactions to which Kitwood refers: *facilitation*, *validation*, and *holding*, all of which make significant contributions to providing the kind of emotional environment that facilitates artistic expression.

1. *Facilitation* refers to the enabling of a person to do what otherwise, without a certain assistance, he would not or could not do. This "interaction occurs when a person's sense of agency has been seriously depleted" (Kitwood, 1997, p. 91). The therapist's task "is to enable interaction to get started, to amplify it and to help the person gradually fill it out with meaning" (p. 91). In the art therapy context, the therapist's experience with materials and projects as a means of evoking creativity are central to such facilitation, especially when reluctance, lack of confidence, and inexperience are encountered.

2. *Validation* refers to an acknowledgement of the subjective world of the person and to responding on the feeling level. This, by necessity, involves a high degree of empathy and an attempt to understand a person's entire frame of reference, even if it is chaotic, paranoid, or has hallucinatory aspects. Naomi Feil adopted this term in her book *The Validation Breakthrough* (1993) in which she adapts the idea of validation to dementia care, teaching the art of communication with disoriented "old-old" people who are struggling to survive (p. 16). The art therapist's unequivocal

acceptance of whatever is created by the patient, at any level of ability, and simultaneous attempt to make sense of the productions, opens the opportunity for the patient to feel validated, "to feel more alive, more connected, more real" (Kitwood, 1997, p. 91).

3. *Holding* is a reference to provision of a safe psychological space where hidden trauma and conflict can be brought out and exposed, without endangering the integrity of the personality or risking the disruption of the ongoing therapeutic relationship. Metaphorically, it is as if the therapist is holding the disparate pieces of the patient together, so that he doesn't fragment.

REGRESSIVE NEEDS

Donald Winnicott (1971) refers to the holding environment as being the essential organizing factor in the emotional development of the child, and this very early mother/infant relationship becomes the paradigm for many of the events that occur in the therapy situation. According to him, in order for the child to develop a healthy internal world, it is essential that the mother have a capacity to "hold" the infant, in a sense insulating him from the invasions of the outside world, as well as serving as a temporary bridge for him between his internal world and the outer world. The mother presents the world to him, giving it to him in small pieces that he can absorb, protecting him from stimulations that he cannot yet tolerate and that might overwhelm him. Anne Clancier and Jeannine Kalmanovitch (1984) describe the process as follows: "The infant cannot . . . distinguish the outside world from the inside world, nor can he at first distinguish between the real world and the imaginary world. The mother must gradually help him to make these distinctions . . . she must not present him too suddenly with fragments of the world that are too large" (p. 13). Judging from observation of the dementia patient, a large part of his experience is of this regressive lack of differentiation of the internal and external, or the real and the imaginary. One wonders if Aristophanes was referring to aged people with dementia when he said thousands of years ago, "Old men are children twice over" (Shenk, p. 112).

Barry Reisberg (Shenk, 2001) coined the term *retrogenesis* to describe inverse relationships between stages of Alzheimer's disease and phases of child development in the areas of cognition, coordination, language, feeding, and behavior. The disease, according to this, is like the unwinding of a giant ball of string that unravels the brain almost exactly in the reverse order as it develops from birth. Increasingly the behavior of dementia patients replicates that of a child before successful separation/individuation has taken place. And while to caregivers the notion that their esteemed elders are intellectually inferior might be an insulting one, the idea of retrogenesis can help them "forge a new understanding and appreciation of what their loved ones are going through"(Shenk, 2001, p. 126).

Observation of the mother and infant as they interact shows her providing just the right warmth for her baby, talking in soft tones so as not to bombard him with noise, holding him if he cries too long, and only gradually leaving him to be alone in short patches of time in order to discover the world. This is the good-enough mothering that Winnicott (1971, p. 10) talks about. In many ways one attempts to simulate such an experience for the Alzheimer's patient, whose internal mechanisms are collapsing and who is regressing to a point where he can no longer count on his own internal shield of protection. As the helpless child depends on the mother for ego support, so the gradually regressing Alzheimer's patient is increasingly in need of this "holding" environment from the therapist. "The therapist protects the situation from intrusion adopting a nonjudgmental, but concerned attitude . . . providing consistency from one session to the next" (Byers, 1995, p. 17). Unfortunately, the therapist/patient relationship differs from the mother/child relationship in pronounced and painful ways. The therapist of the Alzheimer's patient must be a container in a situation in which there will be no improvement, no growth, no development, and no ultimate separation, but rather the opposite. The ability to accept that one's patient will not get better and that there is no significant future to hope for is probably one of the hardest aspects of this work, depriving the therapist of a fundamental, motivating satisfaction.

MIRRORING

Art therapists do more than simply encourage and stimulate the art of their dementia patients; they observe and gaze at the productions, providing satisfaction for a fundamental human need to be seen or mirrored. According to Self psychology, the maintenance of a healthy Self depends on the satisfaction of five basic needs, one of which is "mirroring needs" (Wolf, 1988, p. 55). Attentive gazing from a nonjudgmental and accepting and loving figure satisfies this very basic urge. It was a need for which Narcissus, staring at himself in the water, in love with the image of himself, could find no satisfaction. He looked for himself, in himself, lost in a loop of self-adoration; ultimately, he was plagued with great loneliness, unable to let go of self-love in order to develop and enter relationships with others and to bask in the joy of being seen not by himself but by another. Being seen by the other is what satisfies the basic human desire for relationship. It is precisely such a connection that Alzheimer's patients are increasingly deprived of and which the therapist can partially supply in the art-therapy encounter. Once again we can return to the mother/child relationship to learn about the fundamental importance of early intimacy and how it affects adult life. It is through the loving gaze of the mother that she becomes a mirror for the child's existence, for his "nascent self" (Davis & Wallbridge, 1981, p. 121), and it is through this early interaction that the self-image of the child is being formed so that if he is denied such satisfying and necessary experiences, chances are he may be denied a subjective feeling of reality all through life. The issue of "being seen," which was such a central notion to Winnicott, is particularly relevant in art therapy with Alzheimer's patients because they are given an opportunity not only to be seen in their exterior bedraggled, diminished form, but in their distinct interior world, which is observable on the page. The patient is thus seen beyond his walker, his wobbly legs, and his impoverished verbalizations. The mother gazes at the child; the art therapist gazes at the artwork that is given birth to by the patient. Being seen in this way has an "empowering effect" that "calls forth spontaneity and a trust in unconscious processes" (Thomson, 1989, p. 42).

EGO SUPPORT AND ERODING BOUNDARIES

One of the most significant functions of the ego is to contain the individual, to separate him from the "other," and to provide secure boundaries for the self. This is the ultimate desired outcome of the separation/individuation struggle, when the child comes to terms with the fact that he is not part of his mother, but a separate being. Freud believed that the ego is first and foremost a body ego; that the experience of separateness had to begin in a physical experience. It is when the baby touches and plays with his own body and is touched by others that he learns where his body ends and the outside world begins. Didier Anzieu (1989) talks of the importance of a skin ego, which has a containing function and aspires to envelop the whole psychic apparatus. This is a mental representation that emerges from the interplay between the mother's body and that of the child's.

Tragically, a reversal process takes place in dementia (the *retrogenesis* talked of earlier), gradually eroding this skin ego. Deprived of a protective shield, it becomes more difficult to distinguish the self from the other. Francis Bacon depicts such bodies and faces, with skin that provides them only superficial unity, whereas in fact they seem to have no real internal support to hold themselves together as they bend and lose form and features bleed into each other. As the patient becomes more regressed, and as this crucial boundary is being

Plate 1. A tree.

Plate 2. Three delicate trees.

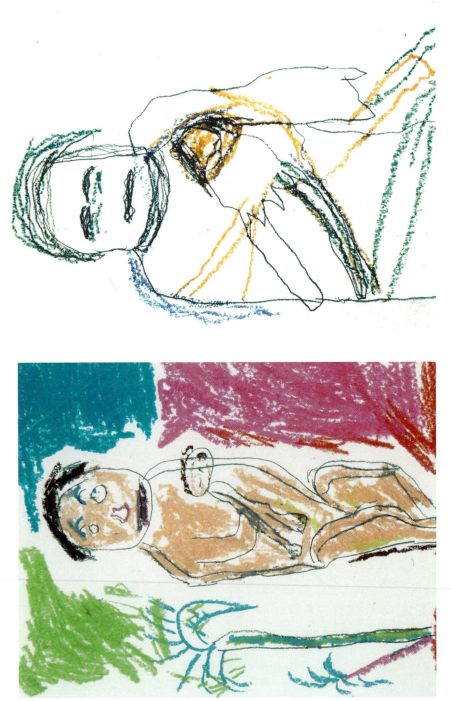

Plate 4. Mother/child, 2.

Plate 3. Mother/child, 1.

Plate 6. Still life, 2.

Plate 5. Still life, I.

Plate 8. Mask on a predrawn outline of a head, 2.

Plate 7. Mask on a predrawn outline of a head, I.

Plate 9. Portrait, 1.

Plate 10. Portrait, 2.

Plate 11. Portrait, 3.

Plate 12. Portrait, 4.

Plate 13. Copying from Henry Moore.

Plate 14. House, 1.

Plate 15. House, 2.

Plate 16. House, 3.

Plate 17. A portrait.

Plate 18. Tanya: Early picture using oil pastel.

Plate 19. Delicate pencil drawing, 1.

Plate 20. Delicate pencil drawing, 2.

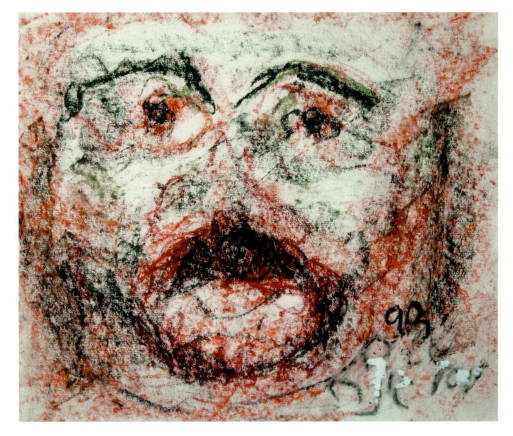

Plate 21. Unpleasant face.

Plate 22. The ship.

Plate 24. The hand.

Plate 23. Demons.

Plate 25. Early portrait.

Plate 26. Later portrait showing perceptual distortion.

Plate 27. Experimenting with art materials.

Plate 28. Anxiety.

eroded, he feels more vulnerable to invasions and more dependent on others to substitute for this failing function of the ego to prevent such invasions. The therapist, therefore, increasingly takes on the role of a mother who supports and helps organize and coordinate the "child's" inner world. Thomson talks about the importance of a temporary giving-up of the discriminating ego, which she calls "oceanic undifferentiation" (1989, p. 47), when involved in a creative process. Unfortunately for the Alzheimer's patient he is actually losing the safety of such a discriminating ego because of the decline of his mental apparatus. For him, the loss is more likely to be permanent, threatening, and even potentially damaging. He cannot risk this adventure into blankness, emptiness, or a state of fusion, and the art therapist must direct activities with this in mind. The therapist will work toward containing, stressing boundaries, clarifying, and reminding patients of their goals and intentions in their work. He will initiate rituals, encourage repetitions that provide safety and continuity, and diminish the chance of unpleasant surprises. The patient needs constant encouragement, guidance, compliments, and confirmation. None of this eliminates the possibility of creativity but only accentuates the importance of structure within the freedom/structure polarity. Schaverien (1992) says, "Frames, by the fact of their rigidity, provide a complement to, and even facilitate, a certain freedom or opening of the space within. Boundaried space permits potentially unmanageable images to be contained" (p. 71). In many ways, the therapist will feel that he is with a little child. In the case of the child, however, the ego support functions as a temporary aid to growth and development, while unfortunately, in that of the dementia patient, it is to help him survive, to provide prosthetic support in a world he has fewer and fewer resources with which to cope. In an O. Henry story, "The Last Leaf," an old artist draws a leaf on a wall outside the window of young woman who lies ailing in her room. By so doing, he ensures that she sees the leaf from her bed each morning, manipulatively providing her with hope and therefore the strength to fight her illness. Having decided that she will die when the last leaf falls, she is nurtured by an illusion that since the last leaf was robust enough to survive the storm, so might she. The drawing sustains her during a period of weakened ego capacity, connecting her with her life force. In some ways the art therapist, too, tries to keep such connections alive for the Alzheimer's patients for as long as possible.

THE NEED FOR RELATIONSHIP

According to Martin Buber (1970), to be human is first and foremost to be in a relationship. In his well-known declarations that there can be no I without a Thou and that all actual life is encounter, he is telling us that in order to feel our humanness, we must be in interpersonally connected. The I does not and cannot exist in isolation. Most psychological and philosophical writings stress the essentially relational aspect of the self, or psyche. Sartre said that in order to exist, people must consort with others or else face an estrangement from themselves at the basic somato-physiologic level. The "nausea" experienced by Rosenquin in Sartre's novel—*Nausea*—is seen as a breakdown of the cohesion of the Self (Wolf, 1988). Kohut would describe it as a regressive fragmentation with lessened cohesion, permeable boundaries, diminished energy and vitality, and disharmonious balance. According to this, the emergence in childhood of the Self, and its sustenance throughout life, depends on the presence of "others" who provide a network of empathic, confirming responses. Without such experiences, the Self cannot retain its structural integrity and will regress to a loss of inner cohesion. Deprived of these sustaining relationships, in a world where one is undervalued, ignored, and unseen by others, the sense of a coherent Self has no chance of survival. Bacon's disintegrating figures can be seen as a response to such deprivation. John Russell (1971) says of them, "What painting had never shown before is the disintegration of the social being which takes place when one is alone in a room which has no looking-glass. We may well feel at such time that the accepted hierarchy of our features is collapsing, and that we are by turns all teeth, all eye, all ear, all nose. . . . Our person is suddenly adrift, fragmented and subject to strange mutation" (p. 38). How interesting that Russell should be talking of the response of "everyman" to isolation, yet this disintegration is so clearly reflected in the portraits made by dementia patients who are not only damaged at the cognitive level but also equally deprived of encounter. At a certain point in the life of a person who has Alzheimer's, the suffering due to his mental deterioration is compounded mercilessly by other losses: of role, sense of importance, and control, for example. But it would seem that the hardest to bear, and the most dehumanizing, is the tendency of those around him to relate to him less and less. The art therapist can provide compensation for such losses by listening to patients through the art, absorbing the meanings of the symbols, connecting with the emotional contents, and expressing interest in the productions. In this way, he provides moments of encounter lacking in their lives, so that even quite advanced Alzheimer's patients feel both listened to and understood, sustained by a sense of humanity and worthiness.

TRANSFERENCE AND COUNTERTRANSFERENCE

The foundation of dynamic therapy is the transference relationship in which the patient projects onto the therapist emotions that belong to significant figures from early childhood experiences. These projections become the basis for understanding how the past colors present interpersonal relations, and within the therapy situation they become an important tool to help the therapist relate to the meaning of current encounters from the patient's internal perspective. Within the supportive intimacy of the art-therapy meetings, strong feelings of relatedness will be aroused in the patient, largely of a positive nature, but they will also include aggressive and hostile emotions. In Chapter 5, I show that the cognitive limitations of Alzheimer's do not preclude this desire, need, and capacity for relatedness. However, these relational capacities are hampered and diminished in the later stages of dementia, when there is a growing confusion of the boundaries between "me" and "the other." As the condition worsens, this differentiation becomes more obsolete, until eventually, there is even confusion at a physical level between what is the patient's body and what is someone else's. Everything becomes part of the same indistinguishable world of objects with no separateness, no difference between being alone and being with another. Under such conditions, transference has no meaning, since there is no "other" on which to project one's feelings, the therapist having become an inseparable part of the patient's world.

However, in the early and middle stages of the illness, there is still sufficient boundary differentiation for the transference to be an important aspect of the therapeutic work. In the art-therapy interaction, these projections are reflected in different ways in the pictures and artwork, which can be understood in the context of the emotional currents aroused by the patient/therapist contact. According to Schaverien (1992), the picture may be regarded as a window on the transference: "Unconsciously the client may paint the therapist into the fabric of the picture, thus revealing the current constellation of the transference" (1992, p. 137).

The transference relationships are not interpreted to the patient with Alzheimer's because of the compromised ability both cognitively and emotionally to make use of such interventions. Intellectually, the connection between past experience and current emotions can be difficult for the patient to absorb. Any painful revelations or opening up of old wounds in order to reveal defenses that have served a protective function for so many years can be of little use. There is no hope for the future, no source of consolation, and little flexibility that would allow for change. This makes interpretations invasive and counterproductive. Nevertheless, the therapist himself can make use of an appreciation of the projections and transference responses that are awakened so that he can understand the patient's internal world. With such understanding, he can make sense of often-bizarre behavior, unravel meaning in the art, and react less personally when attacked with undeserved aggression, rejection, or criticism—or, for that matter, intense affection and the excessive expectations that arise from it. Keeping track of the projections from the patient onto the therapist all help to make the therapist a sturdier container of the emotional world of the patient.

The nature of the transference responses will be influenced by the personal history of each individual patient, but there is a range of responses that appear with greater frequency in Alzheimer's patients that are more directly linked to the nature of the illness. The therapist is almost always a lot younger than the patient, and it can be disconcerting for the aged patient to feel a loss of authority over someone who could be their child, someone whom they still feel they have the right to control. In projecting these "unfinished" emotions toward their own sons or daughters onto the therapist, there are times when the patient can be quite combative, inappropriately rejecting the structure of the patient/therapist relationship. At the same time, since the patient often feels vulnerable, dependent, and needy, the compassionate, attentive, and helpful therapist will evoke primal associations to a parent figure, even if this therapeutic figure is extremely young. Brian Martindale (1989) points out that this final stage of his or her life often comes after long periods of dislocation from grown children and years of loneliness: "Impoverished family situations can often fuel the most intense transference demands/needs from these elderly patients" (p. 70). While being cared for in a sensitive way by the art therapist often "stirs up . . . longings for the idealized much-missed caretaker, daughter/ son," it can also result in feelings of "hate and resentment which can be difficult to bear" (Martindale, 1989, p. 70). This can be confusing for young therapists who themselves may be of an age at which they have adored, functioning grandparents who are the same age as their patients, a reversal of relationships that is complicated to process. Shenk (2001) points out that we regard our children as somehow incomplete people over whom we assume a certain responsibility. To assume this posture over a parent or grandparent, "who stood for a lifetime in a position of moral authority is a sad and sour thing" (p. 126).

The transference onslaught from patients naturally evokes many countertransference responses in the therapist, a mix of emotions that have to be dealt with in order to avoid responding in an angry or punitive manner to unreasonable demands or objectively inexplicable aggression. Strong reactions from one's patients are difficult to absorb dispassionately, especially when the therapist's own unresolved early-relationship issues are touched on by these "attacks" of love or hate. The therapist will have to find a way to separate himself from the feelings of the patient, distinguishing between emotions coming from his patient and those from his own emotional world, yet avoid becoming cold and uncaring. When able to make such distinctions, he will be able to remain close and emotional, yet contain and attenuate the patient's conflicted inner world. Intense emotional demands, depression, despair, anger, and love can be extremely stressful even for experienced therapists, resulting in unconscious anger, withdrawal, and unacknowledged rejection of the needy patient. Unexamined and unexpressed, this can lead to guilt and overcompensation. Therapists can wear themselves out trying to provide the suffering patients with more than the patient/therapist contract warrants. In the attempt to assuage the overwhelming sense of guilt, the therapist might develop unrealistic, grand rescue fantasies and begin to denigrate other staff members because they are not prepared to make sufficient investments. Martindale (1989) points out that the therapist who works with geriatric patients chooses to do so, in many cases, because of unconscious attempts at reparation of disappointments with their own parents or grandparents. Working out one's past relationships through therapeutic work with patients leads to frustration on both sides. When uncontrolled countertransference feelings are encountered, they are best dealt with in regular supervision, collegial meetings, and most of all, in the therapist's own therapy.

In conclusion, art therapy with Alzheimer's disease is well anchored in traditional psychotherapy, in spite of the illness-imposed limitations that create a major difference in depth and quality of experience and diminished capacity for change. Kitwood (1997) points out that psychotherapy traditionally ends when sufficient change has occurred, it begins to consolidate, and it can be implemented in everyday life without the help of the therapist. With dementia this cannot occur, and while some therapeutic work can endure for a time, "there is no point at which the therapeutic work is done. Personhood must be continually replenished; if it is not, relational confidence and good feelings will drain away, leaving a person in chaos and ruin" (p. 99). The work needs to be sustained and even increased as cognitive impairment advances. Kitwood believes that good care has "physiological concomitants and consequences. . . . Good care increases vitality and lowers stress; it provides the very kind of internal environment that is conducive to general health and tissue repair. . . . Bad care devalues the person and so puts the entire organism at risk. It enhances anxiety, rage and grief, and these bring all manner of pathology in their train" (p. 101). The use of art therapy adds an additional dimension to work with dementia because the symbolic expression, in the context of a relationship, is itself therapeutic, giving hope in a world where cognition is gradually failing and language ability is severely challenged.

5

PORTRAITS: THREE CASE STUDIES

To restore the human subject at the center—the suffering, afflicted, fight-
ing, human subject—we must deepen a case history to a narrative tale:
only then do we have a "who" as well as a "what," a real person, a patient,
in relation to disease—in relation to the physical.

—*Oliver Sacks*

The effect of art therapy on the Alzheimer's patient is essentially that of an enrichment of the quality of the here and now. However, there are cases in which
a meaningful therapeutic impact can be discerned over an extended period of
time, in spite of profound disruptions in the memory process. The story of
three patients and of their surprisingly deep therapeutic encounters show that
in some instances, there is a form of knowing and remembering that cannot
be articulated verbally yet is accessible when an alternative path of communication is opened through the language of art. There was little biographical information available about these patients, and during my years of weekly
meetings with them none of them was equipped to fill in gaps in my knowledge of their long histories. Yet through the artwork and by attending to the
symbolic content, I learned to know them intimately as they shared their deep
secrets and longings. This does not mean that all patients with severe cognitive
impairment benefit in the same manner from the art-therapy meetings, nor is
the therapist privy to many such processes on a daily basis. The cases I have
chosen to illustrate can admittedly be deceptive in their neatness and coher-
ence. Many patients with dementia show far less emotional investment, have
less natural talent, sometimes inexplicably lose interest and enthusiasm, and
often cease to attend the group due to illness or a sudden deterioration in their

functioning. But in spite of the exceptional nature of these three stories, they testify to the value of expressive therapy even in the face of severe forms of dementia and are gifts to the therapist from which lessons can be learned.

Working in geriatric facilities can be emotionally taxing, and the experience can involve much anxiety, doubt, and sadness. An enormous amount of effort and energy is demanded of the therapist in order to elicit even small creative successes. The patients' continual complaints and despair threaten to undermine the enthusiastic dedication of the staff, and they make "burnout" a serious problem. The encounters I describe provide some consolation in the face of the daily grind of hopelessness, satisfying the therapist's legitimate need to feel that his investment is justified. Tanya, already in an advanced state of dementia when we began meeting, created a large body of often-beautiful work. Through her images and her skillful use of materials, she gave voice to her need to retain a sense of invulnerability and independence and at the same time expressed her longing for intimacy and togetherness. Adam, a man in his eighties, showed marked confusion regarding time and place and was extremely infantile in his emotional responses. Yet, over the years, he crafted impressive graphite drawings that represented the modicum of mastery and control he was able to maintain, and he smeared gouache paint with abandon, giving life to his feared internal demons. In the case of Simon, whose symptoms of dementia were mild, the art experience evolved into a territory of joyous freedom and spontaneity, resulting in a vast improvement in the depression from which he suffered.

The impact of these stories depends to a large extent on the art they produced, testimony to a world of feeling that the patient cannot verbalize but that exists in spite of severe memory loss. The pictures both illuminate and are illuminated by the context in which they were created and by the narrative of the therapist as he stitches their meanings together. "Outside the context of the therapeutic relationship the picture fades and is flat; a lifeless representation. If I am able to tell the story of the picture and of the way it fit into a series and if at the same time I can convey something of the transference and countertransference, then it may be possible to reanimate the picture in this foreign context. . . . It is only if I am able to engage my colleague by transmitting my understanding of the potency of this particular image in relation to the history of the client, that I may be able to breathe life into the picture in this external . . . cultural context" (Schaverien, 1992, p. 152).

Oliver Sacks is a master at storytelling in which he makes his patients the heroes in case studies that often read like legends. According to Silberman (2002) "the force driving his tales is not the race for a remedy but the patient's striving to maintain his or her identity in a world utterly changed by the disorder." The following stories will show how three such "heroes" used creative work to declare their individuality and produced artwork that turned a light onto their silenced inner world.

Tanya: Daring to Give and Take

All therapists have the fortune, from time to time, to encounter patients who respond to therapy with a display of surprising capacities, justifying the often laborious, daily investment in work. For the art therapist, the rewards of such encounters are amplified because the patient leaves behind documentary evidence of success, art productions serving as colorful reminders of active and creative participation. Observed as a body of work, the meanings shine through and significant processes and transformations are displayed. The experience with such a patient can be likened to the satisfaction of parenting a child who eats well. This is the child/patient who, in taking satisfaction in the nourishment provided by the mother/therapist, is ensuring an equally satisfying experience for her. These patients are not displaying compliance, the domain of the "false self," but, rather, they are using the art materials in their idiosyncratic, personal, and emotional manner while the therapist looks on at the excellent use being made of all that she is offering.

One such experience began for me one sunny summer's day, when a pretty and petite woman, younger in appearance than the many octogenarians in the unit, strolled unannounced into my art room. Slim, fashionably dressed, with a long, carefully braided, blond plait hugging her back, she questioned me about the art room. Glancing disparagingly at the pictures on the wall, asking rather challenging questions, she was sufficiently articulate for me to mistake her for a casual visitor, a relative of a patient, or someone who had lost her way and meandered into the wrong department of our very large hospital. Her responses to a few rather more penetrating questions alerted me to the fact that she was indeed lost—inside a world of confusion, impaired memory, and limited judgment. What she retained and projected was a style that she probably had used all her life, an air of independence, superiority, and disdain. However, in time, this proved to be only a very thin defense against the growing threat of the degeneration of her mind.

Tanya was diagnosed as being in the relatively static middle stage of dementia, still able to live alone, in an apartment close to the hospital, to which she managed to find her way independently each day. This competence was deceptive, as I learned from the social worker who had found Tanya's home in a chaotic condition of neglect and disrepair, and although there was clearly a danger of a serious domestic accident, she could neither understand nor be persuaded of the fact that it was no longer appropriate for her to live alone. Because of her misleading facade, it came as a surprise to see how little she knew about her current life. She could not recall how many children she had, neither their names nor where they lived; nor did she have any conception of the reason for her daily, and what she considered voluntary, visits to the unit. Often she declared her need to "hurry home to make dinner," "fetch the children from school," or rush away because "my mother is waiting for me," all of which were, of course, inventions due to her internally fractured sense of time and place.

Tanya's appearance concealed a world of underlying confusion, anxiety, restlessness, and paranoia and a general agitation that manifested itself in her roaming about the center, entering room after room, looking for something nameless. Initially, she rejected any idea of joining the art group, choosing to come and go as she pleased. The staff humored her through this period, making allowances for her acute anxiety, hoping that after a grace period she would settle down. Nonetheless, my room increasingly attracted her, and eventually a casual, breezy contact was created. She would "pop by" to say hello, complain about her headaches, and share her paranoid thoughts about being robbed, confined, or abused by unnamed enemies. Sometimes she related to me as though I was an old friend she was visiting out of a sense of obligation, while at other times, she would look around the art room with curiosity, then quickly retreat into an air of superiority, not sparing her criticism and contempt for any of the earnest and struggling participants. Finally, one day when we sat quietly alone together, I put a few pages of different sizes in front of her, with a box of oil pastels nearby. With a snooty look of indignation, as though to humor me, she chose a small page and drew a large flower in the center, with some apparently unrelated and unconnected objects around it—a female figure, a sandwich, a smaller but similar flower, and a tiny house—a theme that would become significant as time went on (Figure 5.1). For the short time that she drew, she was quiet and absorbed and seemed briefly distracted from her obsessions. Thus began her love affair with the art experience that lasted for three satisfying and challenging years. Tanya had had no experience with creative work during her life, so that I had little expectations regarding her abilities. However, this first flower, though crudely executed, as well as the following experiments with various materials, convinced me that she had untapped artistic inclinations, natural technical skills in the use of color and line, and a capacity to become involved and aesthetically concerned with the events on the page.

Our twice-weekly sessions usually began with Tanya informing me of how dispensable I was and how rushed she was. Only after clarifying her absolute

Figure 5.1. The first picture. This picture contains elements that would be repeated in many forms over the next few years: a flower, a female figure, and a house.

independence could she enthusiastically invest in her first few drawings, admiring, criticizing, and correcting. This capacity for caring involvement, with apparent emotional satisfaction being derived while at work, is one of the crucial indications that the patient will benefit from the art endeavor. Parallel with the emotional benefits there is also ample evidence of physiological and neurological changes in the body while actively engaged in art activities (Achterberg, 1985; Samuels & Samuels, 1975). Rollo May (1975) wrote of the artist's experience of neurological changes, which include "quickened heart beat; higher blood pressure; increased intensity; and constriction of vision" (p. 44).

All these add up to a feeling of "joy" similar to that of reverie or dream states. Tanya appeared to be drawn into such a state of relaxed breathing and intense concentration when she was involved with artwork.

She insisted on making her own rules and schedule, often arriving in the middle of a group meeting. If there were more than three people in the group, or if any emotional issue was touched on, she immediately "developed" a headache, folded her work midway, and left the room. By conveying the message that she did not need contact or assistance, she inevitably affected the team's response to her, making them feel redundant and irrelevant, and it certainly did not endear her to them. Yet it was clear from many incidents that occurred that this was a defensive pattern, a cover-up for her vulnerability and insecurity, which she felt compelled to hide. On one occasion, on my return from annual leave, which Tanya appeared neither to notice nor to care about, a crisis occurred. She had lost her handbag, or, as she claimed, it was stolen. Tanya was devastated, and in an agitated, compulsive, and perseverative manner, she nagged, accused, and investigated everyone and could not be calmed or reassured. Faced with the inconsolable Tanya, it was imperative that I attempt a more creative intervention, since the entire unit was being persecuted by her loud displays of grief. I hoped that by taking this concrete issue and exploring its metaphoric significance, I might understand and connect with her distress at a deeper lever. She had invested her emotion into an object (much as the artist does into any of his artwork), and I felt sure that this object was the container of certain compelling content that I hoped to address, and in so doing, relieve some of the stress.

"Poor Tanya," I said (also poor me, since I had been accused so persistently of theft, neglect, carelessness, and insensitivity). "You come here only to find that the most precious thing that you own has disappeared." She paid more attention to this than to my previous attempts to calm her.

"No, it was stolen," she belligerently replied. But with a more softened tone, she added, "It had everything in it." Tanya's bag, as with most patients', was practically empty, usually containing nothing more than an often-used tissue, a pilfered crayon, or a dry piece of bread left over from breakfast.

"You must feel as though nothing is left," I continued.

"Yes, it's empty inside." (Was she simply mimicking me, I wondered, or was I on to a real emotion?)

"Empty!" I ventured. "A sort of hole?" And then I groped around to access her feeling state. "I suppose you feel very angry." (An assumption based on her days of rageful outbursts.)

At this, she burst out crying. "Not angry! Don't you see? I'm sad. So sad. I have nothing left. Can't you see that? They've taken everything."

This conversation, without any interpretation on my part, miraculously calmed her. She seemed to have been able to make contact with her sense of loss and impoverishment, which probably was exacerbated by my sudden absence during the few weeks of my leave. She was incapable, both because of her cognitive decline, but also because of her proud and defensive personality structure, to directly express her loneliness and sense of abandonment. Through her grieving about her handbag, she could give voice to this feeling of loss without forfeiting her pride and independence. But at a deeper level, and quite unconsciously, I surmised that the loss she was experiencing was that of the "hole" of dementia. It was this that was eating away all her capacities, strengths, and independence, and into the lost object she poured her grief, crying collectively for all the other losses.

Tanya's pictures, "read" over the three-year span, tell the story of many of her inner struggles and conflicts and their minor transformations. Embedded in the very first pictures were images and themes that she repeated, with many variations, throughout our sessions. These functioned as an alternative, symbolic language through which she could communicate the duality and conflict of her inner world: the longing for closeness and intimacy and the constant struggle to distance and protect her very vulnerable self. Repetition played an important psychological part in Tanya's work, acting as a "method of gaining control over significant and traumatic events" (Stronach-Buschel, 1991, p. 68). Thus, she repeatedly returned to three central images in varying forms, which served as metaphors illuminating this conflict: the house, the close-up portrait and the mother/child couple.

THE HOUSE

The house is a powerful image used by many patients as symbols of the Self. Through this structure they reveal aspects of their experience, with particular personal associations assigned to each of its parts. The exterior of the house signifies the persona or mask—the part that is in contact with the world. This could be thought of as the ego, with the walls serving as both to separate and negotiate between the inner and outer world. The roof corresponds to the mind or head, either sitting comfortably on top of the structure or else presented as a burdensome weight on the fragile walls, in each case the bearer of metaphorical meaning. Tanya spent many hours drawing houses with elaborate backgrounds, using photographs and magazine pictures as the initial stimulus and almost always including a tree or group of trees in the work. In the first representation of a house, in Figure 5.1, it appears in a minuscule but very detailed drawing in the upper-right-hand corner of the page. There is a path leading up to the front of this miniature house, which sends a message of invitation. But at the same time it is very distant, has no door, and is surrounded by a fence, making it quite inaccessible. Only by peering up close can one make out some of the elements.

In a later version (Figure 5.2) more than half the drawing is devoted to the thick forest on either side of a wide pathway that leads to the distant and secretive house, or castle, situated in the depth of the picture. Again we can see this interplay between invitation, which takes up most of the page, and the rejection evoked by the distance of the barely visible house/castle. This picture resonates with legends such as Sleeping Beauty, in which a period of personal arrest predates an internal transformation. Sleeping Beauty, protected by the thick overgrowth, can only come to life after some loving, confirming act from an "other." The loving prince of the legend is represented by the caring therapist in the therapeutic relationship on which we had embarked. It was within the protection of this relationship, as it became more meaningful to her, that certain internal transformations could take place.

In psychic language, windows and doors represent the entrances to the interior world. It would seem that Tanya is unconsciously dealing with her own

Figure 5.2. The house/castle. The entrance to the mysterious domain is deep within the picture, far from the observer's eye.

personal accessibility and her willingness to trust me as a "guest" in her house. Pictorially she represents the conflict through opening and blocking various channels of entry. This issue was expressed repeatedly, in a variety of forms. One picture has the house much closer to the foreground, and this time it has many windows but lacks a door or pathway leading up to it. Three trees are placed in such a way as to partly camouflage it. Without a visible entry to the house, or a pathway leading up to it, it appears isolated and cut off. In another (Plate 14), the house is enclosed snugly by a fence that appears to be guarding its safety. In this picture she invests less energy on the details of the structure itself, paying more attention to the surrounding landscape of mountains, the sea, and an empty field in which the house is situated. A small path emerging out of nowhere leads to the door that is on the side of the house. From the middle of the red roof sprouts a tall thin tree, a living, striving force leaning toward the water, which in Jungian terms is a symbol of life. Once again it is an image of isolation and self-protection placed in a barren landscape, but it is also a reaching out toward life. In Plate 15, continuing the theme of accessibility, we see a house that has no door, is set far back on the page, and is without a path leading up to it.

According to the mystics, the feminine aspect of the universe is a "chest, a house or a wall, as well as an enclosed garden" (Cirlot, 1971, p. 153). Tanya deals with these feminine themes for a prolonged period, expressing her concerns with her femininity and sexuality. She amplifies themes symbolically with various apertures and pathways, metaphoric allusions to her need for privacy and fear of intimacy. In later works these issues are more directly expressed through the female figure that appears with increasing frequency within the house pictures, her size and placement on the page changing the sense of the picture. In Plate 16, the female form is more womanly, but she stands in an icy landscape between two bare trees at the side of a path that again leads to a distant, barely visible house. Tanya appears to be connecting with her frozen sexuality and her existence in a cold and forlorn world.

In Figure 5.3, the figure has the proportions of a child and stands with her back to us, observing the two houses ahead of her as though in conflict regarding the choice of which one to visit or to which one she belongs. One of the houses is in the upper center of the picture, whereas the second is in the far-right quadrant—a minute and distant representation of a house, as in her first picture. While the main figure in the picture is a little girl, the eroticized tree on the left is an expression of her adult, sexualized version of a woman that she needs to camouflage as a tree.

These pictures of the house can be read as successive chapters in the ongoing story of Tanya's struggle with her dependence on me, her therapist, as it

Figure 5.3. A child observing two houses. Tanya represents herself as a little girl, contemplating the two different houses ahead of her. In the forefront of the picture is a tree that strongly resembles a woman's body, reflecting her concern with her female identity.

reflects "the hopes and dreads" of closeness (Mitchell, 1993, p. 15). Like Tantalus, who is never quite able to get to the overhanging fruit or drink the water at his feet, the viewer of Tanya's house pictures (as well as her often-frustrated therapist) is always kept one step away from entrance into the internal domain. This is part of the pictorial dialogue and conflict that Tanya related to throughout her creative process, but sadly, because of her cognitive limitations, there was never any hope that she could come to a form of resolution or integration of the conflict. What she could do was create a symbolic language in order to touch on these internal dilemmas and communicate them to a safe companion in the context of a therapeutic journey. And in this way, by showing me how dangerous intimacy was for her, she was paradoxically creating an intimate relationship; in her cautious way, she was sharing her inner world with me.

THE "CLOSE-UP" PORTRAIT

The "house" motive occupied most of her attention for the first year of our meetings, after which her interest in them began to wane and was replaced by other themes, one of which was the close-up portrait. Tanya repeatedly drew faces of women at close range, often choosing the same photograph from which to copy, without being aware that she was doing so, working and re-working the same themes (Plate 17).

In many of these portraits, the hands are tucked away in pockets, hidden behind the back, or left out entirely as sleeves simply left to end in empty sockets, evoking a feeling of powerlessness and vulnerability (Figure 5.4).

Hands are points of contact and give the ability to caress, take charge, or aggressively punch or hit. All this is denied Tanya's female forms, which portray her own experience as she navigated through a world in which she was gradually becoming more isolated and impotent. The images to which she compulsively returns look concerned and worried. But most significantly, although she uses pictures or photos of adult women as the source of her portraits, in her interpretation, they have youthful facial features and wear childlike dresses that lend them an uncomfortable ambiguity regarding their age. The ambiguity in these woman/child portraits is very much what Tanya conveyed in her behavior when she was present in the art room: she snorted her superior comments with the authority of an adult, yet searched around like a little girl for attention and comfort.

THE MOTHER/CHILD COUPLE

As Tanya became more comfortable in her relationship with me, the theme of the mother/child dyad began to occupy her works. Sometimes, she would add a story to her drawings, the contents of which related to the relationship between the two characters—a lost child seeking out the mother or a child presenting the mother with gifts. These images touch on the emotion of primary relatedness, a regressive emotion harking back to the childhood attachment to the mother before separation/individuation has taken place, when the child is still part of an inseparable mother/child unit. As Tanya became more connected to me, I became the longed-for, caring, mother figure, and she could permit herself more vulnerability, allowing herself to long for comfort and maternal protection. In these dyadic pictures, the face of the baby and that of the mother are almost identical, displaying little difference in age. I would surmise that Tanya was dealing, at an unconscious level, with two different experiences of herself. On the one hand, she was discovering ways to depict the *inter*personal issues of the relationship between herself as a baby, to me, the therapist, as mother. But they also can be read as an expression of an *intra*personal experience, of herself both as mother, or adult woman, and child. In such a manner, Tanya touches on her internal dialectic, blending the two parts of herself into one.

Figure 5.4. Woman/child picture. Both the innocent, helpless facial expression and the absence of hands convey childish passivity.

In Figures 5.5 and 5.6 we see the mother and child as almost inseparable images, the faces of mother and child close together and reminiscent of the tradition of double self-portraits such as can be found in Sigal Avni's (1998) powerful photographs of mother and daughter. A similar twinship can be seen in the double-portrait paintings of Egon Schiele. "Welded together by body language and by a shared outline," the "artist conducts a disturbing dialogue with his other self" (Schroder, 1999, p. 60).

Tanya was incapable of expressing connection to others, or of showing any gratitude, as this would have implied dependence, thus increasing her vulnerability. Her disdain was an attempt to guard against such uncomfortable feelings. Nevertheless, in incidents, enactments, and pictures, she clearly revealed her underlying longing as she increasingly succumbed to the emotions enlivened within the transference relationship. On another of my absences from the unit for a few weeks, I returned to find Tanya sitting alone in the room, drawing, unimpressed as usual by my sudden reappearance, neither commenting on nor acknowledging my presence. Since she was not scheduled for a meeting and

Figure 5.5. Mother/child, 1.   **Figure 5.6. Mother/child, 2.**

Tanya is showing two aspects of herself: the dependent child and the adult mother. The second picture was drawn about a year after the first and shows the signs of deterioration in graphic skills.

I had other appointments, I could not spend much time with her. Later, when I came to check on what she had done, I found her hurriedly putting on her coat, preparing to leave. In front of her, propped up against a vase, was a small sepia-colored pencil drawing of a woman holding a potted plant (Figure 5.7). She had copied this from a photograph in a magazine of a woman looking down at a plant on a table. But in her version, the face of the woman is directed to the observer, to whom she seems to be handing the plant. Under it is written, "To Ruth—with love."

"This is a gift for you," she told me, an act that both astonished and deeply touched me. I had had no indication in all the time spent together that she had even absorbed my name, and I certainly would have doubted

Figure 5.7. The gift. The offering of a symbolic gift: "To Ruth—with love."

that she remembered it from one meeting to the other. This unexpected memory capacity confirms observations that memory is influenced by emotional context; any information that is emotionally loaded has a greater chance of being retained. Achterberg (1985) reports on a study by Lyman, Bernadin, and Thomas in which it was established that the number of images an individual experiences increases during periods of high emotions, as compared to situations of neutral or minimal emotions. The fact that I had become emotionally significant to Tanya helped her to hold on to my name in spite of the generally profound disruptions of memory and my absence for some weeks.

Tanya had connected with warm, internal feelings that enabled her to proffer a gift. In spite of her armored defense of nonchalance and devaluation of the "other," she had found something from within to offer to "another." It was, for her, an unexpected moment of mutuality: a daring act of love. I surmised that the compassionate and containing experience in the therapy room had been internalized by Tanya as a "good object," which now revealed itself in her positive and loving capacity. Small but very significant moments such as these are the sustenance needed in order to work with patients whose capacities for transformation are minimal and whose cognitive abilities are so fragile.

Tanya's choice and use of specific art materials was of major emotional significance in the process and in themselves contained symbolic importance. She used oil pastel for her first attempts at picture making. This material was too coarse, the lines produced lacking the delicacy that she finally achieved when she hit on the far more suitable colored pencils, which she used with great delight from then on (Plates 18, 19, and 20). The detailed and focused work with the fine-pointed crayons and the compulsive filling in of areas with hatched lines were compatible with her strong perseverative tendencies, which she appropriated in order to protect herself from loss of control. The laborious, small, repetitive strokes with which she filled the pages calmed her, much as the quiet, structured scenes of houses, paths, and trees were a way of constructing a less-chaotic environment, a symbolic territory of much-needed tranquility in which she could rest from her agitation and restlessness. But to say this is reductive and devalues the power of the artistic and aesthetic drive. I often watched with something akin to wonder as Tanya worked patiently, filling large areas with her small, sloping marks, which would finally come together as a dappled sea, a never-ending sky, or the patiently constructed tiles of a red roof. After very carefully paging through a magazine and highlighting, with a strip of torn newspaper, the pictures that most interested her, then coming back and comparing, rejecting, and choosing, Tanya would finally commit to her choice with a whispered sound of "Aahh." Taking an often insignificant-looking picture of a house, she would proceed to bring it to life, with all of its details, as though she herself were building it, wall by wall, window by window. In an attempt to understand the significance of this for her, I once took home one of these pictures and, armed with the same colored pencils that she used and a piece of paper of the size she usually chose, I began to draw the house. Disappointingly, the process felt laborious and boring, the work was uninteresting to look at, and I very soon lost the desire to continue. Herein, I realized, lay the essence of the creative act. I had approached the picture technically, wanting to find a way to make it lively. After all, I knew how to do it; I had the skills with which to copy her techniques. I was an experienced artist. She, however, with no conscious knowledge of this process, was taking her liveliness, her internal vitality, her drive and desire, and, using these as her bricks and mortar; she was building her house. The house was Tanya's internal world there on the page, built mark by mark out of an emotional urgency. In the past, I too have been driven by such strong creative forces, but this house did not emerge from my need. I was trying to fake it, to get there by imitating, when in fact one cannot imitate the soul of another. This was a most illuminating moment regarding the essence of the driving force of creativity and its ultimate satisfaction.

Working with Tanya threw very strong light on the potential chasm between two worlds: of the language of words and the language of art, each of which accesses different aspects of the psyche. Judging from Tanya's verbal accounts, one would have concluded that the art room and contact with the therapist were of no significance to her. Her confusion was so great that she was never sure whether she was walking into the room for a session or leaving the room, having already participated. She made it clear that she was not interested in coming to the center, that she was there against her will, that the crayons were not colorful enough, the exercises boring, and the results unimpressive. When I did compliment her on any work, she would look disdainful, call it child's play, and criticize it at length. However, parallel to this was the creation and the content of the images themselves, and they tell a different story. The repetition of certain themes, the changing and developing use of particular materials, her undeniable concentration and pleasure while creating the artwork, the significant symbolic content, and the strong emotional connection with the therapist all underwent discernable transformation over the period of the therapy, in spite of the severe damage to a capacity for new learning. Since she was very prolific, creating a substantial number of pictures in a short time, I allocated one wall outside the therapy room exclusively for her work. This gradually became known as "Tanya's Wall," which she plastered with her pictures, hanging them with care, constantly cajoling the staff to come and admire them. When I organized an exhibition of her paintings, inviting her family to celebrate her achievements, it was as though there were two Tanyas: the verbal Tanya, who devalued the entire event, sneering and criticizing throughout, and the Tanya of the image. This second Tanya observed her works possessively, staring longingly and admiringly at her productions. Language, which had become quite useless to her as a method of communication, had been replaced by the usefulness of the image in providing a means of communication of her turmoil and loneliness, pride and satisfaction.

On a rare occasion of generosity, Tanya took out two pictures from her bulging file of hoarded artwork. "These are for you," she said, in her brusque, off-hand manner. Both of these beautifully executed and delicately colored pencil drawings are now hanging in my home, a reminder that parallel to the ongoing, destructive force of the Alzheimer's, which was altering Tanya's mental capacities, she had had the fortune, through her creativity, to continue giving life to a part of herself. Herein lies confirmation of the words of David Shenk (2001), that the "disease's ultimate mortality should not automatically annul patients' expectations of living the fullest possible life for the longest possible time" (p. 250).

Adam: Peek-a-Boo with Demons

Pictures, when created with emotional commitment, can be a source of great anxiety to the picture maker. It is as though the created work becomes a vessel for much of the feared internal life, which has been split off or denied over the years and now suddenly appears in a truly alive and dangerous form out there on the page. Socrates recognized this long before Freud, when he said, "In all of us, even in good men, there is a lawless wild-beast nature, which peers out in sleep." The problem is that in struggling to bury this wild-beast, we also deprive ourselves of the potential liveliness contained in those very demons.

Adam discovered such threatening presences in his art and solved the problem by covering and smearing the images as they emerged and were revealed to him. In such a manner he could make contact with them, give them expression, observe them, and then get rid of them, safely tucking them away behind smeared, multiple layers of brown paint. It was at the moments of meeting this internal world that Adam became most alive, his whole body awake and responsive, his face bathed in color as he smiled and grunted with primal satisfaction, completely immersed in the experience. After this, at a certain point dictated by some psychic wisdom, he could regain control by eliminating the dangerous material. "It was as if the picture was experienced as magically powerful and highly dangerous," says Schaverien (1992) of such "wild" art. According to her, children are permitted all sorts of irrational fears, whereas adults are supposed to have relinquished them, having learned to mask this internal world, hiding what is feared to be madness. Adam appeared to be playing the childhood game of peek-a-boo, in which the child "looks at what it fears and then withdraws from it by the expedient method of making it invisible, by covering the eyes" (p. 57). He found a way to meet the "beasts" and then, metaphorically close his eyes, gaining control by getting rid of what is most fearful inside of him.

Since early childhood, Adam had dreamed of becoming an artist. Blessed with noteworthy natural talent, he was accepted to a prestigious school of art in Berlin but was robbed of his chance to fulfill his ambition because of burgeoning anti-Semitic laws of Germany. Bookbinding was as close to creative work as he was ever to manage, a profession he adopted and succeeded in all his life. From the time of these creative dreams as a youth until his entry into the facility of the daycare clinic at age 82 as a middle-stage dementia patient he had had no opportunity to draw, sculpt, or paint, as he faced the struggles of a dislocated immigrant and the hardships of poverty. For the first few months of art therapy Adam limited himself to formal landscapes, still lifes, and portraits copied from magazines. He was a man unused to expressing himself and was unwilling to enter conversation related to his feelings, bypassing any inquiry of a personal nature with safe banalities such as "a man has to accept his situation" or "it's no good complaining." Only occasionally would he dare to reveal his grieving for his compromised life's desire, a grief one could even better understand as one observed the powerful effects of the expressive experience on his liveliness. Given a piece of clay, he would, within moments, give birth to a sculpted figure, his old, arthritic fingers delicately shaping expressive features into the well-formed head. He was a joy to watch, pouncing on the bottles of gouache paints, enthusiastically smearing with broad brushes and free expressive strokes, adding layer upon layer of paint to large pages with the little-boy look of glee on his face as he lost himself in the world of color. In spite of the impact of the dementia, Adam required very little stimulation beyond the availability of the materials to set off on extended engagement in artistic activity. His creative drive was powerful enough to survive cognitive decline, difficulties articulating whole sentences, loss of memory, and general confusion. Against all odds, the art-therapy experience provided a means to satisfy a largely frustrated, age-old longing.

But art therapy did more than just satisfy his creative desire, though this is in itself a worthy reward for patient and therapist. It also provided Adam with a language through which he could indirectly express a world of feelings that had been rendered taboo, probably through cultural norms, and possibly reinforced by early family patterns. In the restrained and puritanical milieu of his youth, he had developed into a polite and gentle man with a rigid personality structure. According to Jung (1986), everyone carries a shadow, and the less it is permitted expression, the blacker and denser it becomes. The conscious mind disowns the "negative" aspects that remain undeveloped, denied a life or a voice of their own, and thus become extremely threatening in their chronically repressed condition. Through art, there is an opportunity to safely express, in plastic form, this "shadow," the unseen, hidden part of the psyche, those tendencies whose existence are inhibited and therefore acquire demonic power (Jung, 1964).

This is what Adam brought with force to the therapy, particularly when using flowing liquid paints, which tend to facilitate regressive and cathartic experiences. He would begin with an image formed with great clarity, usually an unpleasant face (Plate 21), threatening form, or fierce beast (Figure 5.8), and then proceed to cover it up, until nothing remained of the original image. He could then leave the room with a sense of control, having gotten rid of the demons as though they never existed, though paradoxically having encountered them in a most vital and engaged manner. Bettina Stronach-Buschel (1991) describes this mechanism in operation as it appears in *Where the Wild Things Are,* by Maurice Sendak. Max, the hero of the story, leaves the safety of his room and goes to meet the wild things, and tames them, not by repressing them but by playing with them and mastering them. Instead of being threatened by them, he is the one who threatens with his powers to encounter and control.

Adam's use of color would also undergo transformation as the work proceeded, beginning with quite vivid and bright colors, which then gradually became muddier until the page consisted of a layer of dull brown/gray, the final result of mixing all the bright reds, yellows, and blues together. It seems that something about the intensity of color aroused emotionality, which he wanted to experience and express, but which he needed at the same time to hide and conceal. None of these many works can be displayed here, because all that exists of them ultimately are page after page of brown paint, a deceptively calm surface area, revealing nothing of the underlying tumult and threat, no part of the vital innards left exposed. The final product is no indication of the lengthy emotional process that the patient went through in order to get there. He clearly had no conscious notion of the process he was undergoing, often talking very concretely and in a slightly paranoid manner about the bad animals hiding in the forest (tigers, monsters, demons, wild faces, or bad dreams), just prior to the destructive smearing. Both appeared to come to the service of

Figure 5.8. The fearsome tiger. The threatening creature roams the forest before being painted over and thus emotionally neutralized.

fundamental needs—to touch on these bad shadow images that reside unexpressed within him, and to retain control of them sufficiently in order to restore the neutral facade.

Adam's greatest natural ability was displayed when using pencil or charcoal (Figure 5.9), graced as he was with an effortless graphic ability and an eye for line, movement, and composition. This opportunity to choose different media was highly significant for the satisfaction of his emotional states. Art materials have very specific qualities and are not interchangeable in terms of the emotional needs of a patient. "An art therapist should be aware of the unique

Figure 5.9. A skilled pencil portrait. A spontaneous display of artistic talent.

capabilities of different media, surfaces and tools in order to be able to offer adaptive solutions to a patient's problems in the actualization of his creative intentions" (Rubin, 1984, p. 8). Wet paints will satisfy the desire for freedom, for the flow of emotions and the meeting of different experiences as one color flows and blends into the other. On the other hand, such experiences can be threatening to those who need to retain control, and they will then seek out, or should be guided toward materials that will satisfy a need for more controlled expression, such as graphite or colored-pencil crayons. Adam alternated between these two worlds of expression, at times permitting himself the freedom to smear and spread color, and at others, returning to the safety of the "obedient" pencil marks. The experience and results of the pencil work was also quite different from the free color work because it was usually based either on a picture that he was copying, a still life that I had set up, or a portrait of someone present in the room. This was work done within the safety of a structure, whereas the work with liquid color emanated from his inner imaginations. Without the containment of rules or instructions, Adam was exposed more intensely to his interior world, which in certain circumstances he found too threatening.

Sadly, toward the end of the three-year period of our meetings, his mental health had noticeably deteriorated, as had the quality of his art. He began to lose bladder control and would often urinate—usually only "leaking"—while he was in the art room. While he was not always aware of it, I suspected that there were times when he did realize what had happened and felt ashamed of and humiliated by the incidents. Adam also had a severe stutter, particularly when he was upset or nervous. One day, he appeared in the art room with a large wet patch on the front of his trousers, dragging his increasingly paralyzed legs with the help of his walker. While smearing paint energetically, he began to share an old traumatic memory of being picked out by a sadistic teacher for stammering in the classroom, after which he was so ashamed that he vowed never to talk in the class again. There was an obvious connection between the timing of this memory of an inability to control his words and the current sense of humiliation at his lack of bladder control, which he could only share with me through talking of his stammer in the past.

Our meetings took on a far richer patina, as often happens in therapy, during the period when the therapy was drawing to a close. Adam's imminent change in living arrangements meant he would no longer be attending the daycare center, and so we spent time preparing for our impending separation. A few weeks before the scheduled parting, after I had reminded him once again that we would soon have to say good-bye, he chose to copy a picture of a man sitting next to his performing monkey (Figure 5.10). He drew

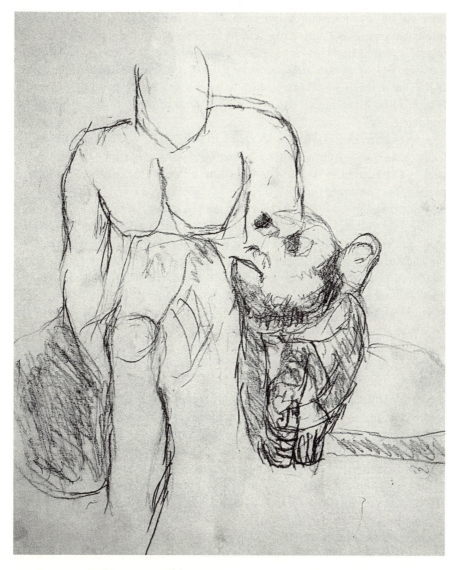

Figure 5.10. The man and his monkey. A detailed image of a monkey staring up with intensity at the large presence at his side.

a cursory outline of the male figure, which in his version was of uncertain gender, with what could be read either as a man's muscular chest or the large breasts of a woman. Most of his energy was then invested in drawing the monkey, stressing the wide eyes staring innocently, pleadingly, at the unrevealing face looming above him. When I asked him what the monkey might be saying to the person next to him, he answered, "Please take care of me." I sensed that this was a reflection of his own growing dependence on me and his fear of abandonment by a face that might be losing its features, fading away, leaving nothing for him to depend on. My impending departure from his life threatened to rob him of a presence of significance, of a mirroring being.

A week later, he stood at the door, shaking my hand and staring at me wordlessly. "You know I want to say something," he finally managed to stammer, appealing to me, it seemed, to find the words to articulate the conflicted emotions in a way that he could not.

Venturing a guess I said, "I think you are sad that we are parting."

"Yes," he said, "I will miss you," which was a declaration of intimate sentiment not easily said by a man taught to hide his feelings. The next time we met, he did a drawing of a man and a woman, very close to each other, holding hands and looking into each other's eyes. He called it "A Meeting between Two" (Figure 5.11).

It is significant that the male and female are nearly the same size and are equally elaborated in distinction to the previous man and monkey couple. I told him that the picture makes me think of the two of us and that it is sad that we have to part. Looking pensive, he took hold of a piece of plastecene and sculpted what he called "the monster." While he was working, I found myself creating a simple female form out of plastecene, which, at a certain point, he took out of my hands and continued to mold for me. Staring at the two completed figures, he began to tell a story of the woman, "that is going away and is waiting for an airplane." When I inquired about the monster's feelings regarding her departure, he hesitated somewhat, cut off the legs of the monster and turned him into a midget. "Now," he said, looking contented with the results, "he can say goodbye."

This brief drama and dialogue contained contradictory messages. Adam, through this sculpture and story, appeared to be telling me about his experience of separating from me. The monster was compelled to transform himself into a midget in order to say goodbye to the woman. At one level he is referring to his feelings for me as monstrous because they are too strong and he has no right to them. Possibly they contain a shameful erotic element that can only be contained by cutting off parts of his being. His great existential fear is the loss of the love object, that he might lose me if he displays this full monstrous part, that I might tolerate only an attenuated version of him. In reality, he himself is in many ways an amputated midget, unable to walk without crutches on his incapacitated legs. But, at an emotional level, too, he is a midget with a limited

Figure 5.11. "A Meeting between Two." A man and a woman share an intimate moment.

and restricted range of permitted feeling, and through the metaphor he shares the sadness of his limitations. He is indulging in a form of splitting, which Schaverien (1992) calls "scapegoating" (pp. 30–61), in which the internal good is separated from the internal bad, which is then disposed of. He smears away any vital, potentially destructive images and castrates the potent monsters. He exposes the powerful life forces, which he considers bad, and then quickly discards them. Thus, without threat to his internal equilibrium, he dares to expose his demon, takes some time to play with the monster, survives him, and then incarcerates him.

It was only through his images and art productions that Adam could possibly express such a range of emotions. He lived an internal life of shame and restriction, but the safety and distancing of this symbolic and metaphorical language provided him a precious opportunity to express deeply conflicting emotions: the fear of his powerful feelings, which appear in the monster, and the longing for connection, expressed in the adoring monkey; the monster's potency, which came through his brightly colored, "beastly" pictures, and his punishment by destroying its liveliness and reducing it to dull muddy surfaces; the brief life of the monster and his timely castration; the love of the therapist, and the self-diminishment and grief at the impending loss. One might well ask what good this experience did for Adam. I could not change the objective reality of his incontinence, address the old traumas in order to provide coping skills, or in any way alter his internal psychological dynamics. However, through the art and within the context of a relationship that had grown over the years, he could experience an expanded version of himself, which included not just platitudes but a palette of varied emotions. This extended version of himself found an accepting, mirroring presence in the therapeutic relationship. It is within the context of this I/thou relationship (Buber, 1970) that we can more fully experience who we are, when we are heard, seen, and accepted by an "other." It is through such a connection that we become meaningful, not just to the other but to ourselves as well. Adam had a weekly opportunity to feel a deep satisfaction as his skills and talents were realized and observed by the therapist, an experience that elevated his sense of self-worth as he joyfully indulged in a language he had been deprived of all his life.

Simon: Coming Out from Under the Covers

Waiting for me in the art room one day sat an elfin man with an eager smile and a sparkle in his eyes. Simon had not been directed to my room but had overheard a conversation about the possibility of joining the art group, and without further consultation, he made his way alone, ready to begin. When I later learned that he had been a bus driver all his life, I imagined him thus each morning, waiting for his passengers to be seated, steering wheel in hands, engine running, and ready to take off. So we took off, Simon with a look of cheerful anticipation, and I, for our twice-weekly art-therapy encounter. While most other participants had to be persuaded to join, reminded of the meetings, or at least encouraged and accompanied into the room, Simon was always sitting in his chosen seat, waiting for the activity to begin. The smile, part grin and part grimace, was, I later learned, a deception, a cover for a severe clinical depression. But in spite of this, from the beginning he radiated a cautious willingness to participate and take chances, so that he experienced many hours of pleasure and produced dozens of pictures over the years we spent together. His determination and hasty engagement were an indication of some very strong life force that lay dormant but ready to flower when given the opportunity.

Simon, married and father of four adult children, had suffered a series of strokes, which left him physically impaired and robbed of his dignity. He hobbled along with the aid of a cane, suffered from a speech impairment that made him a little incoherent, from mild unilateral paralysis, and from partial deafness. In addition, he was in the early stages of dementia of the Alzheimer's type, a condition that often follows in the footsteps of multiple strokes. Both physically incapacitated and increasingly unwilling to initiate any activities in his daily life, he relied on caretakers to bathe and dress him, his physical limitations compounded and confused by the debilitating depression that resulted in almost total passivity. From his wife I learned that he had withdrawn from all conversation, other than pessimistic talk about the pointlessness of life, preferring to "lie under the covers all day long," which I suspected was a sublimated expression of suicidal desires, having lost all his pleasure in living. It was easy to empathize with the profound sadness of a man who, after a lifetime of traveling freely the breadth and length of his country, is suddenly rendered a partial cripple. What age had done to curtail his freedom was now compounded by the attack of an insidious illness, which imposed on him severe physical and mental limitations, binding him to one place and a life of misery.

Simon was cruelly homebound, his life static and colorless, as he strongly intimated in his very first drawing. He hastily painted a picture of a house in the center of the page (Figure 5.12), confined on either side by a tree. The branches on the left side droop in a downward direction, which often indicates despair and hopelessness. Though there is a pathway leading up to the front door, it does not actually meet with the entrance, but rather a little to the side of it as though Simon is conflicted about allowing someone in, cautious about opening himself up to the "outsider." At the same time, Simon came to the room seeking something, something he was not clear about. The path that misses the mark might well reflect an anxiety that he will not find what he came for, that he will not be found, that he will remain alone, and that he will not find a visitor for his soul. On another level, it can be seen as an expression of his experience of being "off center," not quite balanced on his shaky legs, nor internally connected with his self. He himself had lost the ability to enter inside himself, as the black pathway might indicate.

Figure 5.12. The house. A bleak, stereotypical representation of a house painted in black gouache, with a heavy red roof.

In *House as a Mirror of Self*, Clair Cooper Marcus (1995) shows how potent a symbol the house can be as a representation of the self. Simon was unwittingly involved in such a process, touching his soul, representing his innermost thoughts in these drawings. This first picture is a stereotypical image of a house, with its central door, a window on both sides, and a thin trail of smoke emerging from the small chimney. The small chimney and the trickle of smoke released is an indication of how much emotion is allowed to be released: in Simon's case, very little. Other than the red roof, which sits heavily on the black walls and is made with jagged, uncertain lines, there is no color in the picture. It is a gloomy and lonely abode, a true reflection of the emotional barrenness that Simon is experiencing. It is devoid of the liveliness that will emerge as the sessions continue, with different depictions of far more vivid houses that indicate the substantial development and internal changes that are taking place. The rigidity of this first house was eventually replaced with multicolored, dynamic structures built of different levels, with walls often jutting out or indented (Figure 5.13).

These later pictures have a fairytale quality, higgledy-piggledy compositions with multiple doorways, windows, and paths leading into the interiors, roofs of different sizes. These are more personal structures, created when Simon let go of the formulaic house and ventured courageously into his own territory. Often there is more than one house in a picture and trees with varied

Figure 5.13. Another house. A later, livelier depiction of a house created when Simon began to feel greater creative courage.

foliage surround them, while the background is smeared with bright color. The entire effect is one of dynamic movement, both optimistic to a degree, yet with an element of storminess and agitation. The bleak house that at first looked hopelessly rooted in one place gradually becomes infused with movement, warmth, and life.

It is no surprise that he never missed a meeting and was always eager to explore this newfound internal terrain.

A patient's first few pictures usually contain content expressing their basic concerns and stresses, which will be elaborated on in different forms as time goes by. After the hastily constructed first house, which was a theme suggested by me and, one which he continued to develop and enjoy, Simon introduced his second dominant theme of movement, travel, and freedom. The first of this series depicted a bus (Figure 5.14), a colorful and lively means of transport, introducing us to the Simon of the past, who had had an occupation and a role in the community.

This series of drawings expressed his longing for a more vital and colorful way of being, as opposed to the static and limited reality of the present. It is

Figure 5.14. The bus. The colorfully rendered bus, surrounded by birds in flight, conveys freedom of movement.

interesting to note that the branches of the two trees that surround the bus (as they did the house), now reach upward. The wheels are small and unconvincingly attached to the body of the vehicle, so that we sense that he is cognizant of the reality of his inadequate "wheels," or damaged legs. Many times during our work together he was drawn to such images of movement: pictures of airplanes, cars, and buses, as well as of birds and kites, spontaneous, colorful renderings of almost magical possibilities of freedom, to replace his now useless legs. His rendition of a ship (Plate 22), for example, is of a vibrant vessel decorated with a heart on its sail and a large sun in the corner, a source of light, warmth, and hope. These depictions display a growing optimism and vitality, in contrast to that first pessimistic rendition of a gloomy house.

Although his first pictures were simple contour drawings typical of the cautious beginnings of a novice to the craft of art, Simon gradually began a romance of sorts with color, increasingly filling pages with more intense paint applied in thick layers. These representations became a means to make contact with memories and longings for which he was finding less and less outlet in his current life, shamed as he was by his speech impediments and his cognitive limitations. Simon began a series of pictures of masks, monsters, and witches, which were initially entirely cheerful depictions, without any of the later sadness that he was not yet able or willing to share. A struggle began in his work between the rigid, smiling facade through which he contained his emotions and a more angry and pained version of himself that he could not express and that he was probably trying to conceal under the blankets, where he was hiding from the world. What emerged was the enigmatic grimace, somewhere between a smile and a cry, faces plastered with huge, upturned mouths implanted with challenging aggressive teeth.

It is often easier to work with an angry patient than with one who has lost his vitality and interest in living. In our first meetings, Simon presented only a cheerful, smiling persona, one that explains his depression. In the "Grimacing Clown" (Figure 5.15) the mouth is plastered down rigidly, giving the face a frozen expression. A grimace is a mask which "affords no access to character. . . . A rogue may lurk behind an assumed grimace; or an angel may adopt one as a disguise" (Schroder, 1999, p. 64). The neck, which is the place of connection between body and head, is significantly extended, and a black triangular form, probably meant to be a scarf, blocks the flow of contact. This "plug" between his emotional life and the expression of it, is the plug of depression. Gradually through his newfound freedom in the artwork, Simon managed to reclaim some of his identity by expressing a greater range of emotions through his many mask drawings.

The masks and clowns became increasingly angry, confused, and shocked, yet Simon continued for a long time to verbally assure me, as well as himself, that they were optimistic and cheerful, clinging to the older, sterile version of himself. In fact, Simon was terribly sad and angry about his medical and social losses. During one meeting, he told the art group casually, with an exaggerated plastic smile on his face, that his beloved brother had died a few days before. Though I could not be certain about the reliability of his recall, he told us that he had not been included at the funeral for fear that he would be overwhelmed by grief. It seems that the family, reassured by his silence, had not helped him express his reactions either to the death or to having been prevented from being present at the burial. On this occasion, Simon drew one of his smiling clowns, explaining that clowns smile on the outside but are quite sad inside. A dialogue ensued between us in which we talked about the way clowns manage to keep their feelings to themselves. As do many patients who have suffered strokes, Simon tended to confuse laughing and crying, the one easily evoking the other, and I was aware of how much he disliked finding himself involuntarily in tears. It would have been cruel to directly address his inevitable grief, possibly flooding him with uncontrollable emotions. Yet, providing clichés of consolation and encouragement struck me as equally unkind. By dialoguing about the clowns, he could relate to his own feelings indirectly, without threat to the self-protective cheeriness that was concealing his pain. Because the

Figure 5.15. The grimacing clown. The grimacing mouth does not convey a clear emotional state.

defense mechanisms of sufferers of dementia are so fragile, it is always preferable that they invest their energy and emotion in creating images which are then reflected back in such a way that they sense the acceptance and compassion without feeling violated by interpretations that expose and confuse them. When Simon continually drew figures with very thin, stick-like legs, it was his way of confronting painful aspects of his own restrictions in mobility, even though he did not name himself as the "cripple." Many of his drawings of faces contain staring eyes and threatening teeth and are surrounded by heavy black lines. This may well have been a means for Simon to "identify with the aggressor," a defensive mechanism in which one chooses to identify with aggressive and rageful aspects in order to take charge of one's fears and anger and avoid exposing one's vulnerability and weakness. Children who are badly bullied often resort to this pattern. Repelled by their vulnerability, they choose to bully others and thus become the aggressors themselves, developing disgust for perceived weakness in others. Simon might have been making this choice, preferring to experience himself as a vicious monster or witch rather than a pitiful cripple. In an exercise in which I drew the outline of his hand, he filled it in with strong red oil pastel, giving the fingers eyes. From the purple-stained fingernails, he extended colored lines; a thinly disguised attempt at decorating his aggressive intentions (Plate 24).

Simon gradually began to discover the joy of freedom on the page, reveling in territory where he could do neither right nor wrong, where there are no moral criteria for a good or bad picture, a good or bad emotion. His pages filled with flying fish, multiple suns in the sky, dancing figures, faces with disproportionate noses, horns growing from heads, yellow cats, and purple skies.

Without prior knowledge of the principles of the surrealistic school of art, he allowed his spontaneous associations free expression. One has to consider that in an advanced dementia patient, these could be "reflections of perceptual, conceptual and psychological confusion resulting from Alzheimer's disease" (Wald, 1986, p. 74). Simon, however, was in the very early stages of the disease, and it is more likely that in the context of a developing trusting relationship between us, a lessening of inhibitions allowed him to give up internal criticisms and superego restrictions. The varied images and their idiosyncratic combinations more likely represent a visual vocabulary of significant "personal symbols" (Wald, 1986, p. 76). While the results are untrained and executed in a primitive manner, he unknowingly created within a tradition of the Surrealists, articulated by Andre Breton, of a "monologue poured out as rapidly as possible, over which the subject's critical faculty has no control—the subject himself throwing reticence to the winds—and which as much as possible represents spoken thoughts" (Read, 1959, p. 131). In response to his topsy-turvy world on the pages, I introduced him to reproductions of Chagall's flying figures, floating lovers, and cows turned into vases for flowers. I also showed him the primitive paintings of Dubuffet, who uses simple stick-like figures for his densely populated primitive scenes. All of this encouraged a freedom that was denied to him in his restricted everyday life. Through the art, he could give vent to his sense of humor, which previously had been dependent entirely on his now-waning control of language, and he could use the opportunity to express his political opinions, filling the page with verbal associations and puns regarding the upcoming elections and his favored political characters.

The pleasure derived from his "playing" with vibrant color; permission to connect with aggressive, demonic internal figures; the outlet he discovered for his humor and mischievousness; and the opportunity to articulate his views and comments on daily life events began to impact on his life outside the therapy. With markedly diminished symptoms of depression and a renewed sense of independence and power, he soon took to painting daily at home, displaying an initiative and capacity for pleasure in contrast to his presenting symptoms of depression and passivity.

Oliver Sacks (1985) says that "a disease is never a mere loss. . . . There is always a reaction on the part of the affected organism . . . to restore, to replace, to compensate for and preserve its identity" (p. 4). After two years of art activity, Simon informed me with enormous pride that he had changed his signature, dropping his birth name and adopting a new one—Gula. This, he explained, was his artist's name, one that has no meaning but which he was now going to use to sign all his work. Simon had reinvented himself; a new self-image had been born, alleviating his sense of helplessness and worthlessness. He became capable of sustained interest in the artwork, which increased his concentration span and, in turn, his skill in using oil pastel and paint. Hours of satisfaction and pleasure had been introduced into the last part of his life, the world of plastic art having become an important consolation to him. Simon had found meaning and a world that mattered to him, a world he no longer needed to hide away from. He had found a worthy replacement for the desire to succumb to depression and hide under the blankets on his bed.

When the secretary casually informed me one day of Simon's death, I was at a loss for an appropriate response. In busy geriatric units, where death is so much a part of the daily event, this is announced in casual ways. Little time is given to grieve for one's patient of two years, with whom one has met weekly, thought about, and laughed with. Simon's eyes always lit up when I walked into the art room, where he sat waiting for me with a crayon in his hand. The joy of this was more than a moment of personal ego stroking for me, though one never tires of that particular affirmation. The real joy was that I had offered him a language, the experience of which had permitted him to renounce the claim of the clown mask, giving him courage to peel it off during our meetings and risk confronting other, more authentic parts of himself. Once, he announced, stammering his words, "Ruth taught me that the page is my world. I can do what I like in it. She taught me *chutzpah*." I celebrate the fact that Simon died with renewed rights to his chutzpah.

6

*

PROMOTING ART THERAPY FOR ALZHEIMER'S PATIENTS

The notion of art therapy as a valid therapeutic enterprise for the sufferers of Alzheimer's is a relatively new one. It arouses skepticism, criticism, and disbelief in some, while in others, curiosity, interest, and the willingness to contemplate new resources for the treatment of an illness which is still, to a large extent, uncharted territory. This chapter addresses the need and various opportunities that art therapists have to promote the medium. The supervisor has such a role as she guides the new art therapist in her clinical work, addressing surfacing doubts regarding the value of the work and bolstering her professional identity and confidence in her contribution. Art therapists can use their positions in the institutions in which they work to extend their mandate beyond the therapy itself in order to become bridges to the wider therapeutic community, which is often ill-informed about the expressive therapies. If the art therapist is willing to take on an educational role, she can increase the availability of knowledge, remove some of the mystique of the aims and processes of art therapy, and ultimately build a more comfortable existence for herself within a less suspicious institutional setting.

A therapist works not in isolation but within an entire treatment setting. "Our efforts and our reactions to the prevailing atmosphere of the institution will ultimately affect the subtle interplay of patient and therapist. There is a responsibility to understand those currents and make efforts to gather around themselves a supportive group of peers and colleagues to support their efforts to provide an appropriate holding environment for their patients." (Dolginko & Robbins, 1987, p. 117). By explaining and demonstrating their craft, therapists can help create an atmosphere in which they feel more understood and their contribution is acknowledged. As an extension of this, they should consider sharing their experiences and their insights into the power of creativity as a source of well-being with the wider medical community. Workshops for a variety of paramedical professionals can facilitate greater acceptance of the work, providing a service for those who are seeking additional resources for their work. All of this ultimately helps generate respect for art therapy as a worthwhile endeavor; one that can add to the quality of life of the Alzheimer's patients.

SUPERVISION

The importance of supervision for the development of all therapeutic work can never be overstated. The role of the supervisor is a complex and multidimensional one, with a variety of mandates, depending on the needs of the therapist at any particular point in their professional development. For the recently graduated therapist, the supervision will revolve around the basic technical issues of art therapy. The fledgling art therapist will be learning about "the unique capabilities of different media, surfaces and tools in order to be able to offer adaptive solutions to the patients' problems in the actualizations of his creative intentions" (Rubin, 1984, p. 8). The supervisor will guide him as he learns to facilitate creative events, practice the art of "reading" the meaning of the visual symbolic language, and develop the capacity to understand the final art product. The supervisee will develop an understanding of all these fundamental tools of art therapy, which he will then adapt to the specific problems of the dementia patient, developing skills to initiate creative experiences. This knowledge, of an intellectual and technical nature, is often sought by inexperienced art therapists who have not yet acquired the flexibility of matching technique to varying populations, or by therapists who come from other disciplines and desire to include art experiences in their work. Many of these issues are addressed in Chapter 3.

Another role of the supervisor, conditional on already established knowledge of technical aspects of therapy, pertains to professional definition. The supervisor will help the therapist internalize a professional identity in the face of recurring doubts regarding the true value of this work. Art therapists have a tenuous place in the pecking order of the therapies: not quite psychotherapists, even though often they have had extensive psychological education and training, and not occupational therapists, though to an observer, the activities that they initiate can look very similar, and not art teachers, even though they must be well trained in the understanding of the effects, suitability, and manipulation of various art materials. Art therapists still, at times, are involved in debates that attempt to bolster the acceptance of art therapy as an autonomous discipline with its own integral theory, language, and self-definition. "The curious mixture of art and therapy gives rise to responses of suspicion, intrigue, fear, discomfort, patronizing attitudes and on occasion, outright dismissal" (Waller, 1987, p. 197), doubts that are compounded when art therapists venture out to work with the dementia population. In a culture that so favors the young, this can often seem a second-rate endeavor, one that is met with the sort of skepticism that can undermine confidence and create a sense of professional marginalization. Including art therapists in the therapeutic team is still a new idea, and those that have been taken on board will find themselves defending the value of the work. Art therapists do not walk into a ready-made milieu of acceptance and understanding, and part of their task will be that of promoting art therapy and correcting many preconceptions in order to improve their standing in the team. Often, the therapeutic approach of the institution will be quite at odds with the philosophy of the art therapist; the former values calming and pleasant activities, whereas the latter values encounters in which a wide range of emotions, and not always pleasant ones, can be expressed. Such differences in conception complicate the therapist's ability to obstinately adhere to his belief system.

It is in countering this ignorance and doubt that the supervisor faces a major challenge of helping the therapist construct a robust professional persona. It will be the supervisor's primary and continuing task to assist the art therapist in articulating and defending the valuable contribution he can make in bringing art therapy to Alzheimer's patients while giving the therapist the strength to tolerate the difficulties intrinsic to working in the face of illness, deterioration, and death. The road to such self-confidence wends its way through some treacherous territory: devaluation from the outside professional world and persecutory doubts from the internal world of the therapist himself. At a recent seminar for graduating students, none could be encouraged to present casework on art therapy with Alzheimer's, even though quite a few had done impressive practical work in the field. It was not considered sufficiently intellectually stimulating by the faculty or, more importantly, by the students, in spite of the challenging therapeutic work that was theirs to share. It might be that the cognitive impairment of the patient stirs up suspicions that, in a parallel manner, the work of the therapist is less intellectually challenging.

The supervisor also needs to be concerned with the internal world of the art therapist and the way in which it facilitates or blocks the therapeutic work. Without an outsider's vision, or the accompaniment of a trustworthy supervisor, the therapist is in danger of getting lost in his subjective view of the process. Trapped within the proverbial forest, unable to see the dangerous paths or the safe exits, the therapist is in need of an observing eye, one that has a more objective view from the outside, from where the broader picture can be seen. Therapists inevitably have their blind spots, and attacked by an on-slaught of emotional demands, institutional conflicts, and unreasonable ex-pectations, they will flounder without the intellectual and emotional support of supervision.

Certainly this was so in my case, when I found myself caught between my Alzheimer's patients and my increasingly confused mother. I was able to be a better "daughter" to my patients, from whom I could walk away guiltlessly af-ter some hours of work, than to my mother, whose endless questions, confu-sion, and clinging dependency would exhaust me in a far shorter time. When my mother was diagnosed with Alzheimer's disease, it was decided that she would join the daycare unit and take part in my art therapy group. I say "it was decided," whereas in fact no-one really took up the issue; somehow I was con-sidered the expert, and my decisions went unchallenged. Except, of course, that when it came to my own mother, I was clearly not. Spending time with her was always an emotional challenge. Reprimanding myself for not devoting enough time to her, I was constantly trying to control my natural energetic impulse to end an issue and move on. Time spent with her felt like entering a maze, re-peatedly hitting dead ends with no hope of finding an exit, probably a very similar feeling to my mother's, whose looped questions always returned her to the same point. I was constantly in deficit, bargaining with myself about how long I had to stay with her before I rushed off to my busy life.

With patients my experience was quite different, the time spent with them prescheduled and limited in duration. When each session was up, I was free to go on my way, without guilt. They so often expressed gratitude for my atten-tion and devotion, and I was able to derive a sense of satisfaction as they hob-bled out of the room with smiles of pleasure on their faces. The deep disquiet I felt regarding my mother's gradually deteriorating condition increased my need to be more constantly available for her. Working with dementia patients must have been providing partial compensation for something I never felt I did well enough.

It didn't take very long before I realized that this confused mother/therapist role was a particularly bad idea from every point of view, but in the interim it contaminated my therapeutic work, led to general mismanagement, and taught me a worthwhile lesson. It was impossible to maintain professional and per-sonal separation between my mother as a loved family member and my mother as patient. She was completely confused by my presence in what to her was an alien environment, and each time she caught sight of me she would announce to anyone nearby, "I'd like to introduce you to my daughter." This could be re-peated at two-minute intervals, as she showed off, crowing with pride, unable to concentrate on the art activities, confusing the already confused participants of the group with her declarations. Caught up in a flurry of emotions—pity, love, embarrassment, irritation, and impatience—I had the additional problem of responding to the discomfort of the staff, whose professional attitudes to my mother were influenced by my presence. This arrangement did not last very long and was solved by switching her to days when I was not attending the unit. We all have the wonderful opportunity to learn from our mistakes, which can be our best teachers. I fell into the trap of the fantasy of omnipotent capability, exhausting myself in the process, a difficulty that I could so easily identify in new young therapists. Good supervision, and more of my own wisdom to seek it out, would have very quickly put an end to this "wild" therapy, energised by unexamined emotion, rather than by balanced professional judgment.

The supervisor will accompany the therapist as she grapples with some central issues that are particularly pertinent to working with Alzheimer's sufferers.

Processing Therapists' Motivation

The therapist will have an opportunity to examine and articulate her feelings regarding her motivation, often unconscious, for working with this population. The deeper driving forces of the work will often be surprising and quite at odds with the declared professed motivations. Specific questions will focus the therapist on important issues.

Why have you gravitated to work with this population? Therapists often express an ideological conviction regarding the obligation to give time to the aged members of the community. On closer examination, additional personal reasons for the choice relate to early family experiences. There are those who feel that the aged patients fulfill the role of grandparents who were never known because they had died before their (the therapists') birth. Or there are those who had had loving and satisfying relationships with grandparents, and the work somehow provides a consoling satisfaction in the face of the longing for these now-deceased loved ones.

What satisfaction does it provide? The claim of great affection for older people sometimes hides a fundamental desire for the gratitude and innocent love that Alzheimer's patients are expected to display. Frena Gray-Davidson (Kitwood, 1997) believes that the Alzheimer's patient's most fundamental need is for love. The therapist, according to this, has the almost heroic task of providing generous, forgiving, and unconditional acceptance, without any expectation of direct reward. This view reflects the very idealization that I think the supervisor needs to address and challenge, because, while it is sometimes the case that a gentle touch on a patient's back can be greeted with a smile of intense joy, the opposite is just as true. There are times when the Alzheimer's patient is ruthlessly unloving, critical, and unreasonably persecutory, and the therapist who comes to this population with such an idealized expectation of his own capacity for generosity, will find the attacks of rage and endless demands very hard to handle.

What might the therapist be avoiding by working with this population? While therapists talk of the love they have for old people, they also might be avoiding certain difficulties that arise from working with other populations. Some therapists feel insecure when faced with the critical, observing eye of the intellectually robust patient. Although it is annoying to be pursued by the anger of the dementia patient who is clearly paranoid and who needs to be calmed or diverted, a very informed patient with manipulative skills might undermine the therapist's confidence, touching off areas of as yet unresolved difficulties. This preference, based on an understanding of one's weaknesses and strengths, is perfectly legitimate, as is the tendency for some therapists to gravitate to the psychiatric population or to work with autistic or retarded patients for different personal reasons. But it is important to confront the real driving force underlying the apparent ones.

What inner figures, demons, or superego figures are still activating the adult therapist? Therapists need to address the place images of older people hold in their internal world as they continue to exert an influence on them and activate them in their work. These internalized primal figures will drive therapists in unknowing and powerful ways unless they vigilantly watch for their force. Therapists work in the present but hold within them a powerful past. Young supervisees share stories as diverse as that of sexually abusive grandfathers, compassionate grandmothers who took the place of absent or nonfunctioning mothers, or memories of having taken pleasure in tormenting live-in grandparents during childhood, the guilt of which is now hard to placate.

What has the power to disgust and repel us in our work? Therapists who present an idealized picture of the sweet and loving old demented patient will often find it hard to come to terms with certain revulsion at the physical deterioration of the patients—bad body odor and the musty smells of unclean clothes can be disturbing. Unwillingness to acknowledge the threat and fear of living with people who are so close to death can result in a superficial cheeriness or brittle facade, unless such negative visceral responses are confronted.

Addressing such questions, seeking out the unconscious motivations for the work, and uncovering more profound reasons for therapists' satisfaction and frustration, will release the therapist from much tension and internal conflict and lead to a more relaxed and less guarded way of working, benefiting both the therapist and the patient. In the supervision, the supervisee is encouraged to express as much as possible, a range of less pleasant, less "noble" emotions.

These need to be legitimized so that they don't find their way into the work in destructive acting out toward the patient. The investigation will enrich the therapist as she develops the notion of herself less as a skilled technician and more as an emotional human being who is fully and personally engaged in a healing relationship.

Examining the Significance of the Relationship in the Therapy

The supervisor will devote much time to addressing the nature of the therapist/patient relationship. He will help him examine the loving, hating, aggressive, condescending, persecuting emotions that easily well up in the therapy. This is the other aspect of knowledge addressed in the supervision sessions and has to do with the therapist's intuition, insight, creative freedom, personal style, and emotional structure. These issues ultimately affect the texture and meaning of the ensuing dialogue between therapist and patient. It is the stress put on this relationship that casts a different light on the art therapy, rather than the art activities that take place in art classes or within the framework of occupational therapy. The relationship creates the necessary basis for the release of spontaneity and individualism, and its quality can affect the freedom of the art that emerges. This is not to demean the significance of occupational therapy, where, doubtless, strong relationships and their therapeutic results can and do occur. However, in art therapy, the relationship is the central focus of the work of therapy, and when this aspect is neglected by dealing only with concrete issues, great opportunities for more meaningful work can be lost. The Intersubjective approach to therapy argues against the view of one objective observer "healing" the other. This approach is concerned with a dynamic that is set up between two people, through which a third dimension is created in which a subtle, unconscious communication takes place. In art therapy, that third area is partly located in the art object onto which the patient projects his inner world and to which the therapist responds with his own unconscious material. The supervisor's input plays a crucial role in unraveling this subtle dynamic to the therapist. One cannot heal the other in the sense of giving out medicine, but one can be with the patient by truly accompanying him, taking part in his emotional reality, being an engaged listener, and daring to feel his pain, while at the same time honoring one's right, as a therapist, to a plethora of unexpected and uninvited feelings. In order to embark on such a relationship, far more emotional investment and a greater awareness of the unconscious are required, not just of the patient but also of the therapist herself. "A central feature of any context of therapy is the person of the therapist. It is the therapist who establishes what is on offer. . . . Therefore the background of the therapist . . . her beliefs, fears and personal philosophy . . . all communicate and influence the setting" (Schaverien, 1989, p. 147).

The supervisor will help the therapist uncover ways in which her personhood is affecting the therapy and, further, how the therapist's personhood is being affected by the patient. This is the work of uncovering the transference and countertransference relationship. The patient transfers patterns of relating, which developed in childhood, onto the therapist, and the therapist responds to the patient with his own emotional patterns, which are the fruit of his early life and relationships. The therapist has to be helped to differentiate between these projections from his patient and his own reality, otherwise he will be overwhelmed by the love, anger, blaming, and abusing that comes from his patients, uncertain to whom they belong. These need to be separated out from the therapist's own personal emotional history, which is being dramatized in the therapeutic relationship. The influences that the therapist exerts in the session can be very subtle and are often quite unconscious; only by processing his own internal world with the help of the supervisor can the material be brought to consciousness and some control restored.

The experience of Helen, a newly qualified art therapist, illustrates the way a therapist can be released from a certain unconscious internal manipulation once she had understood the interpersonal dynamics between herself and the patient. Helen was to meet with Joel, a handsome, elegant, very well-mannered, and gallant man of seventy-two, who was relatively young for one so advanced in the dementia process. The artwork in the first few sessions was concerned with male/female themes. Joel drew human figures with ambiguous sexuality and faces containing both strong feminine and masculine features, the intermingling of which rendered the expressive images bizarre and perverse. For instance, on one female face he drew a moustache that he erased with dissatisfaction and then redrew, claiming the face was "not manly enough." While it is not uncommon for Alzheimer's patients to draw figures with mixed sexual characteristics, it seemed that for Joel there was a more personal issue involved. He himself had hair and eyebrows that had been colored (a rarity for men in many societies) and many feminine mannerisms, which hinted at the possibility of latent homosexuality. Helen and I spent much time in consultation, exploring whether the disinhibition common to dementia patients was actually allowing Joel to give expression to a latent feminine side that had been too threatening to face in his youth. After all, he had been a high-ranking military officer in his earlier days, a man of social standing and influence in the male world. These issues were central to our discussion until Joel began to flirt with Helen. The difficulty emerged one day when she brought along his latest works, which displayed emotionally barren landscapes in contrast to the lively, if bizarre, male/female figures he had been creating until then. These pages containing stereotypical, childish contour pictures consisting of a brown horizon line with a few red or yellow flowers represented a surprisingly sudden switch in content and style. The question arose whether this was a reflection of deterioration in his condition or a defensive attempt to mask uncomfortable feelings. Helen, as mystified as me, was very troubled by the therapy, and so we investigated what she was feeling during the sessions with him. Had something changed within her that was stifling his chance to give life to more profound emotions, I wondered. With much embarrassment Helen began to reluctantly reveal the flirtatious aspect that had crept into the relationship and how uncomfortable it was making her feel. "I feel as if I'm on a date," she confessed. "He admires the way I look, opens the door for me, and brings me things." Worst of all, and hardest to acknowledge, was the undeniable pleasure she had experienced in his attentions to her femininity and sexual allure, and her anxious attempts to mask this pleasure even from herself. She could find no way to protect herself from her surprising response, other than to become cold, brittle, and a little rejecting. It was not until this shame was exposed and her pleasure in his admiration legitimized and accepted—though not acted upon—that she could work on ways to separate her perfectly natural response from that of her patient's seduction needs. Once she could cease being outraged by her feelings, she could also accept his complicated emotions in regard to her. Having gained more confidence in the fact that she was not initiating or encouraging his flirtation—even while permitting herself the pleasure of his admiring gaze—she could now make place for his lively, if confused, expressions of this male/female dichotomy. His creation of "neutral" landscapes was due in part to Helen's unconscious rejection of and withdrawal from warm involvement with him. After this crucial supervision session, a major internal shift in Helen facilitated Joel's return to his expressive images and deepened the therapeutic process, which he enacted in "romantic encounters" with Helen—dramatized tea-drinking rituals and courtships. Now that she had separated her issues from his, she could quietly participate in this playful activity without threat to her therapeutic stance or to her own feminine longings. And he could give voice more freely to both the feminine and the male sides of his being.

Protecting the Therapist: Avoiding Burnout

In their eagerness to confirm their devotion and commitment, therapists can exhaust themselves, face premature burnout, and ultimately endanger their ability to continue to function. By examining such material, the supervisor will help the therapist avoid doing damage to herself. Excessive rescue fantasies, overly strong empathy, lack of a protective distancing shield, and the risk of being overwhelmed by the suffering of the other: all these are traps that new therapists need to become aware of. Anna, still so eager to get things right, would shamefacedly tell me each time she came to supervision about a patient who refused to invest in any artwork. The patient was a strong-willed old lady who, in spite of her cognitive deterioration, was extremely intuitive about the use of power in relationships. Working on the guilt of the young therapist, she would complain terribly about her loneliness, scorn the art materials, and insist on being taken for a walk. And so keen was the young art therapist, so hopeful that in the coming sessions she could entice her patient into creative activities, that she agreed, while feeling used, abused, ashamed, and helpless. Another supervisee was taking care of a very frail bedridden lady who was only marginally affected by dementia. As the supervision proceeded, she confided that she was succumbing to demands of the patient that were clearly beyond the boundaries of the professional relationship. Remnants of the therapist's childhood guilt, which had not yet been addressed, were giving her patient powerful ammunition with which to dominate her, deprive her of her autonomy, and interfere with her capacity to set limits. Such unexamined forces can too swiftly exhaust a therapist, leaving her with a sense of frustration and failure or, alternatively, result in the therapist acting out, in the form of subtle aggression toward the patient. Only by unraveling her feelings and refusing to succumb to the unreasonable demands could the therapist regain her power and independence and even acquire greater compassion for her patient.

Sometimes the geriatric setting in itself can be the cause of problems. Art therapists, when working with a bedridden patient, might opt to work in the patient's room, bringing materials with them, setting up a small table by the bed, for the duration of the session. This can create confusion in the patient, whose reality-testing is already compromised by the illness. One supervisee managed a year of weekly therapy working in the room of a frail, immobile man. From his confused perspective, in which his early sexist cultural patterns must surely have played a part, he perceived her alternately as a sexual object or as his long-dead spouse. His conversation was suffused with sexual innuendos and expectations that created great discomfort in the therapist. Without the help of the supervision, the therapist's considerable anger toward this inappropriate behavior transformed into a pattern of excessive commitment, which would very soon have worn her out. It was equally difficult for yet another young therapist, who worked in the room of an old lady and found herself being ordered around and asked to do inappropriate tasks because the confused lady related to her as house help. The patient, who on many occasions insulted the inexperienced therapist, calling her a young fool, might well have been projecting an earlier model of the mother/daughter power play onto the therapist, attempting to control her as she would like to control her absent daughter. The therapist, on the other hand, saw in the old lady an image of her beloved granny. No wonder she began to collude with the patient's projections, which she could only deal with when she found the strength and insight to separate her life and needs from those of her patient. In such cases, the therapist has to be helped to clearly define the limits of her professional role and feel less conflicted or guilty about setting clear boundaries while still remaining warm and compassionate.

Touching Despair versus Providing Diversion

The belief system of an art therapist can markedly influence the way in which she handles and influences the content of a session. To a large extent, it is in her hands to facilitate the connection to painful subjects, risking the patient's confrontation with despair and sadness, or to initiate soothing exercises and pleasant themes to reduce anxiety and restlessness. According to Caralyn Johnson et al. (1992), "Responses, including feelings of helplessness, sadness, annoyance, anger and loss of control are not surprisingly those feelings experienced by the patients! To ignore or avoid these feelings serves to thwart the empathic, spontaneous response so necessary to the creative process and for engaging this population" (p. 275). While this is true, the therapist also has an obligation to protect his more fragile patients against the threat of being overwhelmed by internal material with which they cannot cope. Patients with weakened defense systems who are confused and suffer from perseverative, persecutory thoughts need the containing aspect of art therapy, activities that will divert them from obsessional thoughts toward pleasure, refuge, and safety.

The therapist certainly does not have total control over the emotions that emerge in a therapy session, but she can learn, through experience, to use the session for the benefit of a particular patient's emotional state. If the therapist's choice is to avoid eliciting painful issues, it should not be because she herself cannot tolerate despair or because she chooses to exist in a more cheerful milieu or in a more upbeat atmosphere, but rather that in her judgment this decision will be more suitable for the patient's well being at a particular moment.

Importance of Protecting the Vulnerable Patient

One of the most important aspects of supervision is to help the beginning therapist avoid hurting or damaging the patients. This is more likely to occur if a therapist uses his patients to resolve his own unacknowledged and unconscious drives, thus contaminating the therapeutic work. It is perfectly legitimate for the therapist to want to feel that his work is valuable, but when the therapist is unaware of such internal strivings, his work can become particularly self-serving and dangerous.

Sharon, a dedicated, newly qualified art therapist, anxious to improve her skills, met on a weekly basis with an advanced dementia patient. At the beginning of each of our supervision session she would sigh with dissatisfaction. "It didn't go well this week," she would complain, repeating exactly the same words as the week before. Yet the works spread out on the table always impressed me with their metaphorical content that was touching and complex. Clearly a serious transference relationship had evolved with her patient, Marge, and the meetings had become very important to them both. Though the images were graphically simple because of her limited skills, Marge created pictures relating to themes such as envy, competitiveness, and insecurity. However, she somehow always completed the work by adding to or superimposing decorative elements on them, which appeared to cancel out the more painful aspects to which she was alluding. This was unbearable for Sharon, who wanted more of the intense material and as a result pushed Marge to relate to these deeper, underlying issues, when in fact Marge was making it clear that she needed to cover over what threatened to be revealed. Each session we would talk about the need to respect decorative elements, the function of which is to cover up unpleasant emotions, and that vulnerable and emotionally fragile people need to defend against invasion of their secret feelings. Some of Marge's work and comments hinted at an unconscious competitiveness and envy for the young, energetic therapist on whom she had become quite dependent. I suggested that Marge had to defend herself against many potentially overpowering emotions, coloring them with cheeriness and optimism. I tried to reassure Sharon of the value of the work she was doing with Marge, who was suffering from severe clinical depression in addition to dementia yet always came to the meetings willingly and usually departed with a smile of contentment. This haven of pleasure and calm was surely a precious experience for Marge, one that Sharon could take pride in facilitating. Yet Sharon couldn't come to terms with it, smiled at me, and continued to be suspicious that I was only being kind and trying to encourage her.

Any hope for progress lay in unraveling Sharon's countertransference to Marge, something that was greatly disturbing and threatening. Because I was struck by the fact that Sharon questioned the value, for certain patients, of a pleasurable experience, I wondered how she felt about taking pleasure for herself and if she ever allowed herself to enjoy such experiences. What, I asked

Sharon, as I tried to follow her internal logic, are the experiences that you consider supremely important in life? This questioning brought a smile to her face, part revelation and part shame, as though some unacknowledged truth had been exposed, a truth she might have wanted to hide in a way similar to Marge who desired to hide her truths. She confided that for her the ultimate sin would be to be boring. According to this conception, in order to be of value, a person had to be dramatic, intense, exciting, and always active. Sharon described her restlessness at home, where she could not allow herself to ever laze about. She was in a constant twirl of activity, social interaction, and movement, forbidding herself the privilege of rest, of contemplation, or of quiet passivity. And so the penny dropped as she realized how hard it was for her to allow Marge what she could not allow herself. Her punitive superego, which pursued her mercilessly, was now doing the same to Marge. Sharon needed drama, tears, pain, and deep insights from her patient, and anything less than this, was judged insignificant. At a conscious level she knew that Margo suffered from dementia, that her defense mechanisms were rigid, that her condition deprived her of the flexibility needed for real change, and that confronting her negative life patterns was a futile and potentially hurtful endeavor. But Sharon was being driven by her own unconscious patterns. Only when she could understand and face her deep taboo against equanimity and peacefulness, which she equated with dullness, could she begin to give Marge, and patients like her, the pleasurable experience provided by what is, in her eyes, nondramatic art therapy. This was material that Sharon needed to deal with in order to make that step forward as a therapist, particularly when working with the dementia population. Did she somewhere see her dreaded shadow in these patients, flopping about, gazing emptily into space, devoid of passion? Was she coming to face her devils in the psychogeriatric department? Sharon could not accept Marge's right to hesitantly touch on her envy and aggression and then withdraw from it defensively when it hurt too much; first, she had to become aware of it within herself and forgive herself for this need and right.

Processing Age Discrepancy and Dealing with Regression

Inevitably, the therapist working in a psychogeriatric center will be younger than the patient, and in many cases more than a generation will divide them. In a therapeutic context, in which transferential feelings are aroused, the young therapist is often experienced as the longed-for mother. This is a particularly powerful feeling with Alzheimer's patients, for whom reality-testing is impaired. So while the patient must be treated with the respect and honor of an experienced adult, often he will be dependent and needy like a child, the infantile aspect of his functioning exacerbated by the deterioration of cognitive capacities. Much sensitivity is called for in addressing the aged adult and yet honoring the needy child, who is particularly susceptible to praise and comfort and easily wounded by anything that might indicate criticism. For the very young therapist, this dual relationship can be additionally complex and confusing in view of the fact that he might have beloved grandparents who function independently and are themselves still sources of wisdom and strength to the therapist.

The process of regression to earlier emotional functioning that is so prevalent in Alzheimer's patients conflicts with the notion they have of themselves as independent adults. Dementia patients increasingly lose the observing ego, meaning that they are less able to step back and look at an issue both from the distressed internal position and from an objective reality. Deprived of this understanding, the patient has little control and finds himself in a vortex of strong, conflicting emotional needs. It is left up to the therapist to hold within himself these two different perspectives of the patient and to find ways to relate to both. It is no simple matter for a young therapist to accept that he must, at times, take on the role of the parent of a small child when faced with the aged patient. Supervisees, when describing a difficult encounter with an unreasonable patient, will often describe him as behaving like a child. The extreme fears and anger of a two-year-old can be dealt with by the mother through physical holding, reassurance, and distraction. The Alzheimer's patient, in the midst of waves of strong emotion, indeed feels like a child and is best contacted through repeated reassurance and distraction, as well as some physical touching and stroking, which is another version of calming the small helpless child. This is not disrespect, but acceptance on the part of the therapist of the patient's reality and the struggle to suit himself to it. The double perspective that has been lost to the patient has to be maintained by the therapist, the supervisor will sometimes be called on to help the inexperienced therapist contain and tolerate that ambivalence when faced with such a confusing picture.

Supporting Therapists as They Face Death Issues

Working with the aged dementia patient inevitably brings one face to face with the painful reality of the degeneration inherent in much of the aging process, the temporariness of life, and the certainty of death. Anyone who has worked in a geriatric institution will probably have suffered through the death of one, if not more, of their patients. Faced with the death of a member of an ongoing group, the therapist has the difficult task of informing the remaining group members and supporting them through their fears and confusion. One of the defenses against this reality is to distance oneself from the experience, a partially adaptive coping mechanism to protect oneself against some of the tragic aspects of the deteriorating health of one's patients. This can result in a brittle, cheerful therapeutic style that denies the patients their right to express their grief, their anger at the impairment that comes with their aging, or their resentment and jealousy of the younger, healthier staff members. The therapist will never open a window to her patient's deeper emotional experiences unless she has faced the darker sides of life herself. And of course this goes for the supervisor's capacity to do the same. Irving Yalom (1980) believes that therapists must confront death and the anxiety that it arouses; that they must face some of the concerns such as aging, isolation, and death in order to enrich the encounter with the patient and protect against the danger of lapsing into superficial "feel better" encounters. My experience in supervising therapists who work with geriatric patients is that the subject of death underlies much of the dialogue and must be returned to continually. Therapists need a forum in which they can talk about their own fears of death, share any personal experiences they have had with the death of a loved one, and work through their anxiety about how to deal with a patient who brings up issues of death.

CREATING A BRIDGE TO THE MEDICAL STAFF

It is within the institution that an art therapist is working (center, facility, club, hospital, or home for the aged), that he will have the opportunity to be "selling" his profession to the rest of the staff. "Art therapists . . . greatly underestimate the complex nature of the difficulties to be faced in the workplace and the impact these will have upon their work" (Edwards, 1989, p. 167). Furthermore, "contrary to the hopes many of us may have regarding the acceptance of art therapy as a valid way of working with people in need, all too frequently art therapists discover that their way of working is not readily accepted and that they are in conflict with the institution" (p. 168). The problems of recognition and integration that art therapists generally face in institutional settings are even more palpable for this relatively new addition to the care services given to Alzheimer's patients.

RECOGNITION

Art therapy is still widely regarded as recreational in orientation, linked somehow with occupational-therapy activities. Young art therapists, who are grappling with their professional identity, are challenged even further when they move into the field of Alzheimer's, where their role may be seen as that of keeping a large number of patients busy at one time. They are often pressured into accepting too many participants thus diminishing the therapeutic experience of patients who need the personal attention that can only be had in a small intimate meeting. When working with people who are disorganized, slow, and dependent, the number of participants should not exceed six. Yet this might be overlooked because of financial pressures and limited resources, with staff being expected to cover as many patient needs as possible. Therapists might find it hard to refuse the request to include "just these two or three more patients." A young therapist told me that when only one or two of the five permanent members of a group appeared for a meeting, she would feel guilty that she was seeing too few patients and not pulling her weight. A struggle would ensue when a staff member would arbitrarily, and without previous consultation, send an alternative patient, "because today you have a place in the group for other participants" or "because this patient is restless today and maybe she would calm down if she painted." This extraneous decision demonstrates the disregard or ignorance of the process of art therapy and the rules of group dynamics. Similarly, new therapists tend to succumb to the temptation of proving their value and, in doing so, endanger their professional autonomy. One of the tasks of the supervisor is to hold onto the vision of the work, forming a framework, a subterranean network of beliefs with which to nurture the uncertain therapist who is trying to help her patients while she herself, in a parallel process, is being attacked by devaluation or disregard from the larger therapeutic team. Through the support that the supervisor provides, the therapist will internalize a sense of autonomy and worth and find strength to oppose demands that do not fit her professional self-definition.

The Problem of Integration

Not all institutions have the same philosophical orientation as that of the art therapist, and that can add to a sense of isolation from the rest of the staff. New and unfamiliar ways of working with patients in the institution may elicit disbelief, rejection, and devaluation in a staff that is threatened by approaches of which they have little understanding. In these cases, the therapist will have to develop "courage, patience, sensitivity and the ability to compromise" (Edwards, 1989, p. 170) rather than struggle to be the "hero innovator" who has fantasies of changing the entire system and educating everyone in one fell swoop. The supervisor will help the therapist as he struggles through his loneliness and compensatory fantasies of conquest, to the ultimate establishment of professional red lines as he gradually clarifies his rules and expectations. One young therapist struggled constantly against the habit of staff entering her room in the middle of a session to remove an item from the cupboard or to take a patient's blood pressure. Seemingly trivial issues such as these are actually of great significance, giving voice to underlying tensions and misunderstandings, and it requires determined communication and education on the part of the therapist of the needs of a group for privacy, peacefulness, and continuity. Often, a colleague's refusal to cooperate, even after many explanations and requests, indicates a measure of unconscious aggression and envy toward the "alien" therapy. Therapists should be encouraged to present their views and work at staff meetings as well as to volunteer to demonstrate their work through workshops with the staff. This can raise awareness as well as satisfy the underlying curiosity and envy for what medical staff possibly classify as secretive and fun activities going on behind closed doors, while they are working very hard at "more serious things."

While therapists face many difficulties resulting from the lack of recognition in the institutional setting itself, other problems arise from the art therapist's own uncertain self-image, and these need to be bolstered in the supervision sessions. Art therapists can only fight for recognition as an independent profession when they have come to the self-recognition that will help them define their roles. Art therapy has an advantage over the verbal therapies in that there is a visible testimony to the work that has been done, and this has great persuasive power when trying to show its therapeutic value. It is this concrete evidence, rather than explanations about what art therapy is, that should be made use of as the art therapist faces the burden of promoting a serious and accepting attitude to her work. Over the years I have witnessed art therapists present casework without showing the actual art productions of the patients. Such presentations, in the presence of a willing audience, seem to miss the opportunity to promulgate the power of the medium, which is, after all, about images, not words. The most powerful approach involves either presentation of case histories using slides or providing the participants with a mini creative experience, using their artwork and their responses as a basis for theoretical explanations.

One other powerful means of revealing the effectiveness of the art process to the therapeutic team is the art exhibition. Whenever a patient had created many paintings of a sufficiently impressive quality, I organized an exhibition for this work. This is not to say that I place less value on the more primitive, graphically simple, and unimpressive works of the more confused patients, but simply that the exhibition has to take into account an audience who will be more concerned with the results of the art and less concerned with the therapeutic process that I regard as the core of the endeavor.

With the participation, where possible, of the artist/patient, a number of pictures can be chosen, signed, and dated and then framed simply with construction board, all of which enormously increase their artistic presence. On the day of the exhibition all the patients of the facility gather, with family members, recreation and paramedical staff, doctors, and the head of the department. A short biographical account of the artist/patient may be prepared and read to the audience as an introduction to the event, with the patient present as the works are pointed out and the artistic effect of the creations and the means used to achieve the results are talked about. When I have held these exhibitions I have, where possible, made links to the works of well-known artists, showing the use of similar materials, themes, color combinations or styles, demonstrating the universality of the artistic drive and process. On occasion I have included a creative experience for the audience, involving them in some way with the use of color or images. For instance, at one event, I hung up a very large sheet of paper, prepared six large pots of bright paint and a selection of paintbrushes, and invited audience members to come forward to make a mark on the page. Once the first brushstroke appeared, thick paint dripping downward, volunteers cautiously began to contribute their brush stroke. Some could not be stopped once they had begun to freely smear the inviting white page with color, while others contributed no more than a frail and cautious circle or line. But liveliness ensued as the head of the department dipped his brush and made his mark with what looked like the same reticence and ultimate satisfaction as the slowest dementia patient. This was immediately followed by a patient pushing her walker steadfastly ahead of her, snailing her way to the pots of paint and carefully finding a place on the page, close to his, for her bright color. These events were a wonderful confirmation for the patient who, though confused, was always aware at some level that he was the center of this happening.

Hugging bouquets of flowers that family members bring, and smiling as they recognize a piece of biographical information, the artist/patient enjoys an undeniable moment of affirmation. The families, too, are usually overwhelmed with the impressive pictures, observing aspects of their loved ones with whom they had lost all touch as the disease progressed. And, finally, these events can at least partially satisfied the curiosity of the rest of the staff, provide input about the abilities of the patients, and help the therapist feel less marginalized and part of the institutional team effort.

At a certain point in the progression of the Alzheimer's disease the medical profession has very little to offer in the way of therapy. Medical practitioners should, however, be aware of the paramedical care available that increases the quality of life of people for whom there is no cure. Although there is, as yet, no scientific proof of the validity or cost-effectiveness of the work, art therapists need to expose their craft to doctors interested in the available care-centered options. The hope is that these doctors may become advocates of such services so that in the future, through their influence, more such programs will be incorporated into therapeutic settings. I was given the opportunity on a few occasions to present my work to the medical profession when students specializing in geriatric medicine were being exposed to a range of adjunctive approaches to Alzheimer's. It is a daunting mission to communicate the importance of art therapy to fifty doctors, who are trained to approach the condition from the medical, physiological, and biochemical point of view. What chance, I sometimes worried, did I have of convincing them the advantage of an endeavor as anecdotal as art therapy, which is connected with values, ethics, and humanism and in which the dialogue is more poetic than rational and based on intuition and belief, not on scientific proof?

What I attempted was to give the participants an opportunity to use art materials, a small taste of a creative experience from which I could later more vividly extrapolate the theoretical explanations, and a basis on which to relate to the slide presentation that ended the session. I gave the doctors small cardboard pages, pencils, and containers of oil pastel colors and invited them to spontaneously draw a tree. Choosing a few of the more expressive results, I showed them how any image is, to a certain extent, a self-portrait and will contain aspects of the creator. The nature of the contour line (unconnected or broken, as opposed to one continuous line), the pressure of the pencil or color (very light pressure as opposed to lines pressed deep into the page), the placement and size of the image (large and centered, or a small image hugging the edges), the choice of foliage (one large continuous crown, or small detailed leaves), the attention to specific details (concentration on the texture of the trunk, or use of an unusual color), the noticeable absence of important features (trees without foliage or lacking roots): all these are significant in that they convey symbolic information about the subjective world of the person who created the picture. What I tried to display, based on the participants' emotional responses to this limited project, were important principles regarding ways to respond to art products in the therapy situation. For instance, one of the ways to avoid an "artist" later regretting that he might have unwillingly revealed private content is to avoid interpretive invasions of pictures by limiting the remarks to the image itself. One might point out that the "landscape" is lonely and gray, that the "tree" has sensual lines that indicate sexual longing, or that the "sky" is stormy and unquiet. Implications of the "artist's" personal needs expressed through these images can be articulated very discreetly, if at all. Some of the doctors could more easily identify with the creative experience of patients after they had undergone this experience themselves. I used the doctors' responses, sometimes critical and cynical, as examples of what the patients often feel when presented with pages and colors. I was never sure how much of this demonstration penetrated or convinced, but I remain certain that there were at least a few doctors, and that has to be enough, who will in the future suggest art therapy for their patients. Having personally seen how an image can communicate meaningful material, some at least may see the value of having an art therapist on their team.

WORKSHOPS

I have also held workshops and experiential seminars as another way to promote the power of art as therapy. These were attended by art therapists, occupational therapists, social workers, and psychologists, all of whom worked in the geriatric field, were curious about the tools of creative therapy, and wanted to experience the medium for themselves. Through the workshop they could investigate deeper personal motivation for wanting to work with dementia patients and examine a range of authentic emotional responses to them. The more courage the therapist can muster in order to acknowledge the darker sides of his feelings, the less he will have to resort to denial and pretense, which are both energy-consuming. These unconscious motivations are dangerous when left to activate us outside our awareness and control. Experiential workshops can help us face these hidden internal dramas and take control of them by dialoguing and negotiating with them instead of being controlled by them. Following is the outline of two models for workshops.

First Workshop

Aim. To access figures from the past that have been internalized and continue to unconsciously activate the therapist.

Warm up. After an introduction regarding the broad aims of the workshop, the participants are invited to think back to their childhood and focus on one memory connected with an elderly person. This might concern someone close, such as a grandparent, or someone distant who has left a strong memory with either positive, or negative resonance. In cases where grandparents had died before their birth, I suggest a more recent memory or, failing that, I suggest constructing a fantasy of a longed-for or feared grandparent or recalling a character from a book or film. Participants are invited to break into pairs and share their story with their partner but are encouraged to be their own censors and only share what is comfortable for them.

The activity. Clay is divided in chunks sufficient for every member of the group, and a selection of instruments for sculpting is provided. Each person is given a piece of heavy cardboard (or some equivalent material) on which to place his completed works. Although the instructions relate to working with clay, it is best to prepare an alternative medium, such as gouache paints or colored crayons, in case there is a member of the group who is resistant for any reason to touching the clay. The personal tastes and anxieties of group members must always be respected and not forgotten in one's creative enthusiasm. This regard for personal choice acts as role-modeling for the participants, emphasizing that the attraction toward or repulsion from any particular art medium is part of the creative dialogue. One particular medium can contain important emotional content, irreplaceable by another. It would be hard to express intense anger using colored pencil crayons, whereas providing a patient with a ball of clay that he can break into pieces, pound with a hammer, and form and reform into different shapes, is far more likely to give release to that emotion. However any reluctance must be honored, at the same time as one is taking it into account as an issue worth investigating.

Each participant is asked to create two figures in clay—one old and one young. These can be abstract forms, animal figures, or parts of human figures. These possibilities are elaborated in order to open up a greater spectrum of associations and ideas. I suggest that while they are thinking of the figures they might recall the stories that they shared with their partners. When they have finished their works, I ask them to lay the two figures on the boards in relation to one another. Placing them in this way provides a concrete, physical representation of the relationship between the young and the old figures and provides metaphorical material that will later be processed.

Sharing and processing. The works are placed in the center of the circle for sharing, and the group leader helps to connect each story and creative work with issues related to internalized "old figures." In order to focus on relevant issues, guiding questions are asked, such as "On which figure did you begin to work first, the young or the old?" "With which figure did you enjoy working more?" and "According to their physical positioning, what is the relationship between the two?" The responses usually are surprising and enlightening. In one case, the young figure was standing behind an old, chair-bound figure, which led the participant to question her ability or desire to make real contact as opposed to hiding, unobserved, behind the helpless patient. In another work, the two figures were the same size and stood side by side holding hands, revealing a sense of equality and mutuality as they faced the world together. Different issues were raised by the varied configurations and in each pairing, resulting in valuable insights for the participants.

Sample of one participant's insight. Sarah was an occupational therapist who had a very powerful memory of her grandfather being in the hospital when he was dying of cancer. He had asked to see Sarah, who was at the time only nine years old, choosing her from among all his grandchildren to be with in his last hours. She had not been allowed to see him during his slow deterioration, and what she witnessed now, only days before his death, was harrowing. He gasped for air, his body functioning only through the assistance of intravenous needles and an oxygen mask. She stood by his bed helplessly as he grasped her small hand with his long emaciated fingers, repeating lovingly, "My Sarah, my Sarah." Unable to contain herself, she slipped away from his bedside and stood alone outside the hospital doors, trembling. Sarah also shared her childhood experiences of neglect by extremely narcissistic and self-involved parents and the sad absence of any caring adult figures in her life, except for her grandfather. It was the loving relationship with him that had served as a rare confirmation throughout her youth. Recalling it with the group, she found a new dimension through which to understand her dedication to working with the old and demented, for whom her heart softened with compassion and affection. I pointed out, on the other hand, the negative power of her early experience to drive her to an overzealous work ethic. The strong memory and the regressive emotional work with clay had highlighted her attraction to geriatric work; as if, at some unconscious level, through working with the aged or symbolically attending to her old dying grandfather, she could reclaim parts of this loving experience. But when, on occasion, she faced ingratitude and rejection from a patient to whom she had devoted time and care, it was hard for her to tolerate this with equanimity and she found herself retaliating subtly with her own rejection. The driving force behind her work, the search for the loving older person in her life, was undermining her ability to stand back and separate the hostility of a frustrated patient, from her own primal need for love and reassurance.

Second Workshop

Aim. To process the countertransference responses of therapists to their geriatric patients.

Warm up. A large sheet of paper is hung up and the therapists/participants are invited to free-associate and offer words relating to thoughts and feelings about the aged population with whom they work. Initially, the words tend to be of a positive nature, such as loving, gentle, soft, and wise, but then one member of the group might risk introducing a more negative adjective or association, which will set off a stream of words, such as boring, loss of beauty, grumpiness, bad odor, unreasonableness, doddering, and so forth. If the group remains with only positive associations, I might participate and offer one negative word in an attempt to legitimize a wider range of responses and less-defensive associations. From a large selection of pictures and photographs of old people that have been stuck onto cardboard, participants are each invited to choose one that interests them, attracts them, or arouses any emotional response. These are fairly large pictures of the same size, collected from newspapers, journals, and photos, in which the old people are either alone, with a partner, or in a group (such as a family setting) and express a variety of moods, such as cheerfulness, contentedness, sadness, grief or loneliness.

The activity. Each participant sits alone with his "old person," creating biographical details, such as name, age, place of birth, family situation, and profession. These details help to define and evoke a fully rounded character with a personality, history, and social context. The participants are invited to write a story about the person in the picture, relating to what is happening at the time, what happened preceding the moment depicted, and what will happen subsequently. The stories are given a title that is helpful in focusing on the most prominent aspect of the story for the creator. Sometimes the title is quite at odds with the apparent content, and this, too, can help when trying to unravel the meaning of the work later, raising questions of suppressed conflicts or paradoxical responses. A picture of an old lady sitting alone in a bare room was curiously titled "My Happy Life," and much discussion between the group members and the creator of the work revolved around this confusing title. Was the loneliness tolerable because of the pleasurable memories of her happy life? Or did the creator of the story herself resort to denial in the face of such apparent isolation at the end of life? The implication of these possible alternative responses was the material through which the participant could then choose to examine and further explore her own attitudes to her work. Finally participants are given a choice of a large selection of materials (gouache, oil pastel, clay, etc.) and asked to create a work that relates to any issues brought up in their "story."

Sharing and processing. Participants break into pairs and share their experience with their partner. These stories are often of a very emotional and private nature, and it is much easier for most people to share them in the intimacy of a two- or three-person discussion. They then return to the circle, and are invited to share whatever they choose with the group. At this point, the group leader can give more time to those few people who want to deepen their investigation. They are encouraged to make connections between the stories their clay work and their work with aged patients in order to clarify the motivation of the therapist for his work with dementia.

Sample of one participant's insight. Helen was an experienced occupational therapist who worked with dementia patients with inspirational dedication. She was compassionate and intuitive about the needs of the patients and understood the symbolic meaning of their confused communications, and they thrived under her care. However, observing her with the patients, I was surprised and disturbed by the way she related quite differently to the older men as opposed to the women. With the men, she smiled, hugged, laughed, and joked, often in a manic and inappropriate manner. When she spoke of any of them it was usually in an exaggeratedly adoring tone. They were, by her account, all "sweethearts, good men and clever guys." As if, having become demented, all nastiness, sadism, and grumpiness were eliminated, and they had turned into pleasant, two-dimensional cartoon characters. I wondered about this, since the demented male can often be aggressive, sexually infantile, demanding, and downright difficult. Her one-sided view, of which she seemed completely unaware, puzzled me. Then Helen took part in the workshop on the theme of countertransference. She set to work with utter concentration, rolling, smearing, and pounding the clay—the medium she had chosen for her work—in a way that participants in an art group sometimes do, diving blissfully into the creative world, sighing and succumbing to a deeper realm of consciousness. When the time came to clear up, it was hard for her to give up this creative, unboundaried expressive space. Appearing terribly impatient to share her experience when the time came for processing, she excitedly told a story about her beloved grandfather in what I again recognized as her very manic and cheerful manner, adding that she felt the same love and affection for the men in the unit as she did for her grandfather. Her images in clay were that of a pool of water with an upright log nearby. When the members of the group pointed out the strong sexual associations of the image, she paused in surprise, the mania subsided, and she gradually became pensive, subdued, and sad. She shared the story of her childhood relationship with her father, in which there had been a fair amount of sexual inappropriateness and a lot of humiliation and unhappiness. Her beloved grandfather had taken on the parenting role, becoming the object of love and a source of security. But her grandfather was a morose man and, according to her description, suffered from depression. Helen had become locked into the role of entertainer, cheering him up with her laughter and attention. Without her clowning and gaiety, she was always in danger of losing him to his depression and withdrawal. She had never dared face the negative side of her grandfather, toward whom anger or criticism would have meant risking her childhood security; thus, she had limited her role to that of the pleasing entertainer. This was only a moment of self-realization, but it gave her the opportunity to face the reality of a cheerfulness that was born in another era and was no longer appropriate or necessary for her survival. Without facing these early family patterns, she ran the risk of wearing herself out in her efforts to gain the love of her late grandfather, who reappeared again and again in the guise of her male patients. Only when she could take a more three-dimensional view of her grandfather would she be able to experience the less lovable sides of her patients, accept the existence of their negative traits, give up the need to entertain them, and even risk losing their affection.

LOOKING AHEAD

Art therapy is not an exact science, and therapists are constantly on the lookout for new explanations, new ideas, and new methods. Art therapists attend workshops, listen to lectures, observe human nature, postulate connections between events, read literature, share poetry, and constantly come up with new stories regarding the way people function, why they are sad and dissatisfied, and what would make them feel more fulfilled and contented. When they find a story that makes sense, and when they observe that it works, it behooves them to tell it in the hope that others will use it and contribute to more lives of Alzheimer's sufferers. The art therapist who has chosen to work with this population has an opportunity and obligation to tell his stories and to promulgate his beliefs, his experiences, his successes, and his ideology regarding this work, demonstrating to the therapeutic community the creative needs and spontaneous abilities of even of the severely damaged.

1

✳

A PERSONAL STORY

Three years have passed since my mother's death. Very gradually, imperceptibly, memories of her as she was before the illness return, giving pieces of her back to me. I long for the power to dim the shrunken image of her in the last, humiliating months. If I could press rewind as one does with a video and magically return to the beginning, I would see her grow taller, more full-bodied, and more active. She would wear a pink skirt with a delicate floral pattern, and a beautifully pressed white blouse in soft cotton. She would smell sweet, as she used to, smile a lot, and try hard to please. I would see her in the kitchen, where she spent much time preparing for the family, willing us to come and eat, drink, and taste her latest goodies. I miss that woman, masked for so many years by the more recent, insular, frightened, and confused version. My mother's life ended with her curled up in a little ball, her fingers pressed to her face, responding to nothing, only occasionally groaning like an infant. This is how I had last seen her, days before I left for a short vacation in the United States. As I was about to board an airplane in Denver, my mobile phone rang and I was informed that my mother had died. Mercifully, I thought. Peace at last.

This was the end of her long struggle with Alzheimer's disease, a personal experience that enriches my understanding of the cruel and lengthy process of unraveling that Alzheimer's disease causes and is the emotional impetus for writing about an essentially professional experience. When, exactly, the deterioration began is hard to say. I have some home movies, taken many years ago, showing her when she was young and full of vitality. I also have a more recent one, taken at a family celebration during which I recall she had gathered up all the pretty paper napkins from the buffet table and stuffed them into her bag. Greeting one of my wealthier acquaintances, she had taken the opportunity to

offer her a job as a maid, "Part-time, you understand—just some daily cleaning and an hour or two of cooking. I pay really well," she assured her. Yes, there
was even humor involved, but right now I am still unable to watch these
videos. What they are likely to fill me with is regret—the very common feeling
that I should have done more and some grandiose wishes to have saved her
from the humiliations, helplessness, and dehumanization that the last stages of
dementia bring about. Personal experience teaches a quite different lesson
than does a professional one, permitting neither the distancing nor the potential intellectual escape of professional roles. While working as an art therapist
I learned, firsthand, what it is like to witness someone one loves slowly transformed into another, often alien, being. I knew the danger of finding oneself
forgetting the once-delightful being that a mother or father, sister or brother,
once was. I became guiltily aware that I was able to provide my patients with
generosity, compassion, understanding, and, above all, patience, which eluded
me when I spent time with my mother, for whom I felt increasing irritation.

Beginnings are hard to locate: significant moments hide within the dynamics of easily forgettable daily events. Without the thread of Ariadne, one withdraws from the labyrinth on different paths from those on which one enters.
Try as I might, I cannot ascertain if there was any connection between the
early stages of my mother's mental decline and my decision to work in a psychogeriatric unit. The alterations in behavior that appear at the beginning
stages of Alzheimer's disease are subtle and develop gradually, so that by the
time the illness is fully acknowledged, years have passed. During this period,
the earlier relationships are altered and a family member, once so familiar but
increasingly unpredictable, blurs the past and makes it impossible to recapture
where it all commenced. Was my mother perceptibly ill when I became involved in my work with Alzheimer's? She had always had an unreliable memory, always been absentminded, and suffered most of her life from varying
degrees of depression. Looking back, it seems that it was only the intensity of
these aspects of her personality that were changing during those first few
years.

At a professional conference in Tel Aviv many years ago, I met the head of a
geriatric unit, who expressed interest in having an art therapist join the team.
Curious about the use of art therapy with different populations, I agreed to
visit and observe the multidisciplinary approach taken by the unit. The con-
cept was the provision of a range of activities and therapies so that each patient
could take part in one of many options according to his individual interests or
tendencies: music therapy, exercise classes, dance, theater, storytelling, and occupational therapy among others. The man whose joy in life was music could
join a music-therapy group, listen to tapes in a corner of the large common

quarters, or play the piano. A dynamic old lady would not be coerced into "playing with children's toys," as she called the paints and clay dispersed around the art room. "Business," she extolled, "that's what I like. Money and business." She was far more likely to benefit from the group that met daily to discuss newspaper articles and current events.

How much of my desire to contribute, I wonder, was already influenced by signs, premonitions, and fears that my mother was soon going to be part of such a program? My complete misunderstanding of her process of deterioration, as well as some harsh thoughts, are documented in my diary, in the scribbled notes about her slow journey away from the world.

"I have discovered that there are aspects of my mother that I truly dislike," I wrote, not yet suspecting that it was about her illness that I was speaking. "She stares at me angrily. Cross and accusing. Is she irked by my professional success? Jealous? I'm fed up. It's no fun to be around her." I cringe with guilt as I read this. The world must have begun to be confusing for her, things beginning to make less sense; she was regularly staring into people's eyes in order to calm her increasing paranoia. "I'm going to end up like Chaim," she says. "You'll have to kill me before I get there."

Chaim, my mother's brother, had died in a state of dementia. I couldn't bear to hear this, because I didn't know how to reassure her and because it was evoking anxious thoughts I wanted to avoid.

Those first signs, instead of arousing my compassion, brought on anger. One day, sometime in those shady years before final acknowledgement and diagnosis, my mother called on me for assistance. Always rushed for time, I made myself available one afternoon to help her divide her small collection of diamond rings and bracelets and a few trinkets studded with semiprecious stones. These hardly constituted a major treasure, but she wanted to share the pieces among her children, to avoid the possibility of dissension after her death. An admirable act of wisdom, it seemed to me. With a proprietary air she poured the shining trinkets from the velvet pouch that she had taken out of the safe, relying on my help to make a fair division. She luxuriated in the hours we spent together, while I watched the clock stingily, tormented by the thought of other obligations. She was concerned about the relative value of each item, who would prefer semiprecious stones or gold and silver, and who deserved the ultimate gift, the diamond wedding ring she had inherited from her mother. Given that I had my own agenda, jealousies, and greed to deal with, these were Solomonic decisions I was being asked to make. Trying to put aside my resentment that others would be sharing in my mother's jewelry, we spent hours sorting and resorting, until we came to a resolution, laying out three separate piles. She asked which of these I wanted for myself, something I had avoided thinking about, so as not to bias the division. Though reluctant to say, when she pressed me, I made my choice. "Well," she declared, and I suppose this was the moment when I should have realized that some part of her was not functioning adequately, "I never said I would give you the ones you want. I will make the decision for myself in the future." With that, she mixed up the entire collection, carefully returned it to the velvet bag, and tied the cord triumphantly. But my mother was not by nature a spiteful woman, so, did I feel sorry for her? Did I feel concern for her defective judgment? No, I felt helpless, outraged, and, in no small part I suppose, suffused with primitive emotions related to sibling rivalry and jealousies of long ago. For weeks I indignantly recounted the story to all and sundry, casting my mother as sadistic, manipulative, daft, and heartless. All these might have been marginally true, but what I didn't acknowledge was that her emotional life was already contaminated by dementia.

My diary notes reflect the growing realization of serious deterioration, as do the noticeable changes in her drawing abilities (Plates 25 and 26). "My mother is losing her mind. And making us all a little crazy too. I can't bear to say 'Alzheimer's.' There seems no point in having her diagnosed. I know the route. Poor Mom! Poor Dad! Poor all of us." Later, "Yesterday Mom came for lunch. Danny [my grown son] brought her a cup of coffee. She thanked him politely, scratched around in her nearly empty black purse, and handed him a coin. She must have been giving him a tip. To laugh, or to cry?"

The history of the jewelry continued when years later I was once again called upon, this time in a conspiratorial whisper, to "help her keep them safe." By this time, she was well into the middle stage of the illness but had many lucid periods, and she was by no means without a fluctuating capacity for logical thought, limited as it was by her damaged short-term memory. She took out the small parcel, this time wrapped mysteriously in layers of paper towel, crisscrossed with sticky tape, reinforced with various-sized elastic bands, and kept hidden in the drawer by her bed. Confiding to me with appropriate insight that her memory was unreliable, she asked me to attach the name of a future recipient to each item. Fulfilling the request, this time far more rapidly than before, I returned the parcel to its hiding place, rewrapped and bound. That night I tossed and turned sleeplessly, tormented by my irresponsibility in refusing to accept the fact that in many ways my mother was a child who needed to be protected and could not be depended on, not someone you trusted with valuables. But those jewels seemed to represent her last vestige of dignity. She had lost so much, and this pouch contained something she still owned, that was hers alone to give to others as she chose. Through them she retained a certain sense of power, clung to remnants of her old self—the giver, the generous woman of years gone by. Nevertheless, toward dawn I decided to retrieve the jewelry that same day. I told myself she wouldn't even be aware they were missing, she would have forgotten their existence already. When I returned I was faced with an empty drawer, and while my heart sank, I was hardly surprised. To this day, I am puzzled about the fate of the velvet pouch and its contents. She might have thrown it in the toilet, put it in the trashcan, or given it to the household help. Anything was possible. Did she miss her treasure? I can only surmise and say I think she did, in an intermittent, confused, and unarticulated manner. I suspect she was often struck with the notion that something was missing and that she must find it. The what, where, and why, she surely couldn't know. What a tormenting sense of loss, when one has no cognitive ability to comprehend the connection between events, when one lives in a world devoid of logic, not sure what one is looking for or where to find it, and thinking that someone must have taken it. Without even knowing what "it" is. The sense of inexplicable loss is pervasive with Alzheimer's victims, which surely accounts for much of the cycle of helplessness, anger, and paranoia.

Caretakers stand by, helplessly watching significant aspects of their loved ones being extinguished. In her youth, my mother had been passionate about fashionable clothes. There were times when she could be seen admiring herself shamelessly, swiveling in front of the mirror, adoring her very high-heeled shoes, sniffing mightily at her attractiveness. She had been particularly proud of her sizeable collection of dramatic hats, adorned with ostrich feathers, sculpted flowers, or cheeky lacy veils. But when we were preparing for my daughter's wedding, the shabby array of clothes in her closet seemed to be a metaphor for her declining mind. Nothing remained in it that would be appropriate for the occasion, and having not yet absorbed the extent of her mental failure, I took her to a store to choose a new outfit. This turned into a nightmare for her, as she was faced with the multiplication of stimuli, the bombardment of strange people, and the questions she could not answer. The simple act of taking off her clothes and trying on unfamiliar ones was far too complex for her to coordinate. Having finally given up on any useful input from her, I chose a well-fitted, bright red, two-piece suit that was pretty and cheery, even though I knew without question that my mother had never worn this color. She had loved the cool desert shades almost exclusively, yet this is what I chose for her, as though with her Alzheimer's she had lost her intuitive attractions and enthusiasms. The suit hung in her closet for the weeks before the wedding, causing me great discomfort as it reminded me of my insensitive choice. Each time I visited her, she would call me to the room, point to the unidentified object, perplexed, and say, "This is not mine. I don't know who put it here, but it's not mine. It can't be. I don't even like this color." As forgetful as she had become, this was constant. The suit was not hers and never would be. When the night of the wedding arrived, she fretted and fussed and showed such distaste for the alien garb that she ended up wearing one of her old, shabby beige dresses. Shabby, but her color, and one in which she felt comfortable. The continuing stress and the exhaustion of trying to make sense out of the nonsensical dulls the sensitivity even of those family members with the best intentions. Mishandling ensues, further increasing the patient's distress.

I went down this mistaken path again when the strap of my mother's handbag broke. Without this ancient, now-torn leather handbag, she refused to even go to the bathroom. Watching her hug it to her chest with the strap dangling at her side, I couldn't contain my shame. What would people think of my apparent neglect of my mother? So I bought my mother a new bag, and she was distraught, pacing and searching, staring in surprise at the strange object that I had tucked under her arm. When I acknowledged defeat and returned the tattered bag, she clutched it like a toddler's security blanket, once more in safe territory.

My bulging diary continued to serve as a confessional while I watched my mother's failing mind affect her being.

"Come, I need to talk to you," she whispered yesterday, beckoning me into her bedroom. I don't know for how long she will manage a life at home. I dread the next phase. Don't want to think about it. Hunched over to protect herself against some dark, unseen force, she is secretive and suspicious in a way she never was in her younger days (or was she?—it's all becoming fuzzy). Plotting, complaining, and blaming, she sat on the bed sharing her worries with me about the untrustworthy characters in her life. Among them, and chief culprit, is my father, her husband for life. Years of justified anger against him have been now transformed into confused rage and desire for revenge. "I'm going to leave him," she declares unreasonably (she can barely find her way to the bathroom and back). "I'll find an apartment and go. I can't take it anymore. He doesn't want me. I have no place here." And then, with poetic clarity, she continued. "I am nothing." Looking around at the objects in the room, she added, "I am not a lamp. I am not a bed. I am not a sweater. I am not even a . . . a . . . fish. Look. I am nothing." And then, head bowed with helpless grief. "He is trying to get rid of me." This blend of fantasy, exaggeration, and deep truth is heartbreaking. She's right of course. Notwithstanding her diminished intellectual capacity, she knows at a deep level that her husband indeed wants to be rid of her. This truth that she has lived with throughout her life has become more intense as she becomes more difficult to live with. She's restless, more passive, more dependent, and clinging. And now she has no power at all with which to fight this reality. We sat in her bedroom that in the old days she used to adorn with rich paintings, branches of fresh cut bougainvillea propped in unlikely containers, colorful throws and plump pillows on the bed. Once, one would have seen baskets of her collections: of stones, beads, shells, and pieces of oddly shaped metal. She used to gather these on her daily walks through the city, her back firm and straight, her stride optimistic. Gone are the days when I used to come to visit between work hours, needing to rest for an hour or two. She would bring me a cup of tea, with a cookie on the saucer. Her face lit up with the joy of serving me— "My daughter," she would say with pride, "my daughter often comes to visit," I would hear her in the next room, showing off to friends, but quietly so as not to disturb me. Today was different. We sat together in the dull gloom of burned out lights, partners in her tormented world of enemies and plots.

Many moments of dilemma and indecision will overcome those who take care of Alzheimer's patients as the long-familiar person changes inexorably in unpredictable ways. Failing capacities and unexpected new needs demand readjustment by the caretaker, and errors of judgment are unavoidable. One such miscalculation of mine was to include my mother as a patient in the geriatric unit in which I was working. My overwhelming grief when my mother was first officially diagnosed should have been a sufficient warning sign of the lack of wisdom in trying to combine the role of concerned daughter and professional therapist. Preparing myself for her extended interview with the psychiatrist, I breezily confirmed my relaxed readiness to be present, as I had done with many patients in the past. This, in spite of the kind warning of the psychiatrist that "some people find this quite difficult when dealing with a family member." How shocking it was to realize the great gaps in her knowledge and ability to comprehend, remember, or articulate. Her failure to answer the simplest questions was the most painful. My mother had retained a fairly stable social facade, with admirable skill at hiding her confusion, but at this point there was no escape. Sufficiently aware so that she could sense this was some sort of test situation, her anxiety was palpable when asked how many children she had. Panic-stricken, she looked at me, whispering, "This one . . . ," but she could not continue with the mathematics of the answer. Excusing myself on the pretext of needing a cup of coffee, I hastily stepped out of the room and, observed by the staff with whom I worked daily— consulting, supporting, dialoguing—I sat in a helpless heap and wept. My professional experience and intellectual understanding was no help in facing the rawness of pity and desire to protect her against the insult of being revealed in this diminished form. My mom!

In this diary entry, I detect the nagging voice of doubt regarding the wisdom of combining these two roles:

Mom has begun attending the Alzheimer's unit and has joined my art therapy group. Maybe a mad decision? Am I taking on more than I can handle? Not enough that I'm her daughter? Now I have to be her therapist? She follows me around adoringly. She's clearly delighted to be in my company, but she's so confused to see me in this strange environment. When I leave the room to attend to some small matter and return after a few moments, she is thrilled all over again. Clapping her hands with joy, quite unaware that only moments have elapsed since she last saw me, she asks once again, as though for the first time "Darling, what are you doing here?" Her face as radiant as a little girl who has won a first prize. She repeatedly announces proudly to the other patients that I am her daughter. They, on the other hand, look confused, cross and resentful. What to do?

What I did was to very soon reorganize the schedule so that I was not working on the days when she attended the club, as she called it. However, I am eternally grateful for the fulfilling years that she had in this setting, when she could no longer find a place for herself in the world of the intellectually robust. Again, from my diary:

Mom is clearly gifted artistically. What a pity she wasted all of that talent. She had a wonderful sense of aesthetics, but she always discarded and devalued her endeavors before anyone else might do so. It seems that it took her illness for her to drop the self-criticism that in the past had never quite allowed her to invest in her creativity. A paradox indeed. Suffering from this relentless cognitive decline, she can now be so easily persuaded to fill pages with her swirling, gentle, colorful lines, choosing her colors like party favors, regarding the finished product with love and appreciation [Figure 7.1 and Plate 27].

That scowl of self-hatred that I so disliked seeing in my childhood years has now been replaced with a smile of contentment. She stares into people's faces, looking for something inexplicable, and then draws portraits, some distorted, some bizarre, some with suspicious or angry eyes, filled with anxiety [Plate 28]. But then there are those that are beautiful, the lines so fluent and gentle and sensitive that I am certain they reflect a deep, personal quiet and integrity. How ironic that she seems to have come to terms with her limitations and to accept at last who she is.

Figure 7.1. A delicate still life. A drawing in pastel by my mother.

At the center, she seems to have found a place in which Dad, probably for the first time in his life, cannot compete with her, though he has told me he would be willing to give a lecture to the staff on the philosophy of aging. He's longing for a way in, but not through dementia. Living in his shadow for so long, Mom has always been less than him; always audience rather than main actor. Now at last, she has the satisfaction of being received uncritically, with acceptance, warmth, and compassion, when he drops her off each day, as one does a child to school. She belongs somewhere. At last, she has found a place to be herself in an uncompetitive way that she never had before. Talk about the secondary gain of illness!

My curiosity draws me to look at the artwork she is doing on days I am not at the center. I notice she is struggling recently with ways to sign her pictures. She always finishes her work by signing her name, something very few Alzheimer's patients do. Her difficulty seems to be in committing to a definition of herself. Sometimes she writes Cyla [her commonly used name], or Cyla Natas [her married name], or the same in Hebrew. Other times she tries "I," or "myself," or "me." In one of them, she had signed "me" and then underneath it, "I think." It is as though she's seeking and discovering, in all different forms, an identity other than that of an appendage of the too-colorful man with whom she shared a life.

Recently, the drama group decided to enact parts of *Romeo and Juliet*, allowing the patients to elect the characters from among themselves. Mother was chosen to be Juliet (Figure 7.2). No longer present during the time she attended the unit, I was nevertheless invited to the grand performance. I was so proud of her. She's always been coquettish, feminine, and a little flirtatious; now she was adorned for the part with a selection of colorful long necklaces, scarves, and a bouquet of artificial flowers, in which she appeared to feel delighted. The actors had to be reminded fairly regularly about the role they were to play, as they intermittently lost track of the reason for the strange garments in which they were wrapped. Not Mom. She was perfectly comfortable in the role of a woman in love, who had somehow to seduce the handsome Romeo. She showed no confusion. At one point she sidled up to Romeo and said, "My husband has gone to London for a few days. Why don't we spend the night together?" Nothing could have prepared me for this moment of clarity. Dad has indeed gone away, but in his absence, she has been inquiring and nagging, constantly and mercilessly, to know where he has gone, why he has gone, and for how long he has gone; but mostly, when was he coming back. And now, with such utter ease and recall, she informed Romeo that he has gone to London, and that she is quite available for a tryst.

Figure 7.2. Mother, the coquette. In the role of Juliet.

In the later stages of Alzheimer's disease, my mother became almost completely dependent, unable to control her bodily functions, and dramatically confused, which was very wearing on my father who was taking care of her with impressive kindness, but was, himself already in his late eighties. She had begun to indulge in dangerous activities, turning on the gas without lighting it, tasting dangerous cleaning liquids, and strolling away from the apartment. We made adjustments for this, baby-proofing the house, locking the front door and removing the key, putting sharp objects up high, and making sure that cleaning materials were out of sight. My father, clearly worn out, decided that she would be better off protected in an institutional setting. Reassured by the manager of the residence that within a few days she would feel comfortable, safe, and happy, my father, her husband of some fifty years, checked her in one morning. He filled a small case with a few simple items of clothing, stacked them into the Formica cupboard by her bed, and then left her to spend her first night in her new home. All day I was obsessed with the unbearable thought of her alone in this new environment. At nine in the evening I decided to check that she was tucked into bed, as was promised. Quietly, I tiptoed into the large common area, in which the patients sat during the day. The unpleasant mix of odors of urine, pureed food, and disinfectant, familiar to anyone who has spent time in such institutions, increased the atmosphere of gloom and loneliness. As my eyes adapted to the darkness, I saw her, standing in the middle of the deserted room, staring into the dark, her eyes darting around in all directions. She might as well have been dumped all alone on a desert island, for all she could make of her surroundings. Clutching a floral plastic cosmetic bag in her hands, my mother stood trembling, alone, and frightened. Catching sight of me, she moaned, "Darling where am I? You've come to save me. Thank God you are here." Her body still weak and shaking, I guided her to my car and late that night returned her to my understandably reluctant father, who agreed to continue the exhausting task of taking care of her at home. It was not to be for very long.

Not that all the richness of her ailing mind had been wiped out, as, for instance, she displayed to me on the day we went down to the sea to watch the sunset. Mother had always adored the stones and shells and shiny pieces of old glass that piled up along the shoreline of our beach. For this reason, I took along a plastic bag so that she could collect some to take home with her, much as one does for children. At my suggestion that she choose a few for herself, she bent down and simply stuffed the bag with whatever lay in a circle around her. She had lost that discriminating eye for texture, shape, and beauty. I had so wanted to please her and couldn't contain my disappointment as we wearily got ready to leave. Trudging our way back from the sea, plastic bag in hand, she turned around to face the glorious orange sunset and sighed, "I wish I could take home all the shells from the beach." This was a consoling sentiment to my ears, coming it seemed from the more sensitive parts of her being. And then she added, "I know what. When someone asks me about my shell collection, I will say I have many more, but I store them on the beachfront. All of these," she continued, still holding on to the thought, sweeping her hand across the horizon, "are mine. I don't have to take them home with me at all." I knew she would not be connected with that internal place of beauty and wisdom for long, and that sadness, combined with the thrill of her poetic sentiment, filled me with an aching melancholy.

So many times I talked to bewildered husbands, wives, or children of a recently diagnosed patient and quietly consoled them when their worst suspicions were being confirmed, gently touched sad shoulders as they shook their heads in dismay. I knew what still lay ahead. How different this contained professional compassion was to that of my private personal response when my mother was diagnosed. I, too, knew full well what her ever-increasing symptoms connoted. I didn't need to hear, clearly articulated, that she had "Dementia of the Alzheimer's Type." I knew what still lay ahead. Unfortunately, we cannot distance ourselves with the consolation that Alzheimer's only happens to a certain "other" population such as the poor, the uneducated, or the unemployed. The story of Ronald Reagan touched many hearts as we witnessed the deterioration, due to Alzheimer's, of one of the most powerful men in the world. We have seen film clips of the mythical Rita Hayworth in the last years of her life, with the lonely, vacant look of the advanced Alzheimer's patient. Iris Murdoch, the prolific prize-winning author, and Willem de Kooning, the great American abstract expressionist painter, both ended their lives in a state of dementia. The beautiful, the rich, the powerful, and the creative—none is immune to the devastation of Alzheimer's disease. Many of us fear what lies ahead . . .

Some months before her death, after a visit to the residence, I wrote,

Today I took a tape recorder to the home. I want to preserve her voice for later. I sang some songs. Tried to get her to sing along. I sang "Happy Birthday to Mom," and she smiled. Sang a few of the lines. She looks so tiny in the wheelchair. Her body is stiff and spastic. She looks into my face but barely registers. I held her hand. It was so thin and frail, and then I felt her press my hand. I was ridiculously happy. I want her to know who I am. To register my presence. I sat next to her and caressed her back. I put my head against her cheek, so longing for her acknowledgement. I asked her if she liked my hand on her back and heard her whisper, eyes closed, "It's very good." A miraculous gift of recognition!

Could I not have been more tender, gentler, and kinder to my mother? I have a fantasy that had I known and understood what I do today, I would have done it differently. Such useless questions only serve to whet the appetite of the voracious superego, waiting to punish, reprimand, and fill one with regrets! Alternatively, we can at least use the old stories as guidelines for the future: therein lies the hope, and that is how our failed pasts can be put to good use.

AFTERWORD

Do not go gentle unto that good night,
. . .
Rage, rage against the dying of the light.
                                    —*Dylan Thomas*

People often remark that one must have a lot of strength to work with Alzheimer's patients. I understand that to mean they think it is a great burden to contain such sadness in the face of the many limitations and inevitable decay. In fact, there is a different challenge that is more relevant, a different strength that is called for. The therapist sustains a belief in the value of his work in the face of grave disabilities, certain deterioration, and only minor creative achievements. In spite of all of these, he maintains the enthusiasm to light up whatever remains alive and trapped in the patient. Without this, the work cannot succeed. With other troubled patients, the therapist finds a way to spark their vitality through the art materials, a project, a story, or guided imagery. When he has lit the spark, he can sit back and watch the creative work unfold. With Alzheimer's this is not so. The spark needs to be lit and relit, the patient reconnected and reawakened, the vitality hooked time and again. The patient's own memory and cognitive abilities are not enough to keep the work going. Too often he lacks energy, initiative, confidence, and desire. Only a far more active guide can lead him to the path of his remaining creativity. I have worked with many populations and have found that there is a level of exhaustion after leading a group of Alzheimer's patients, a great deal of sustained energy called for on the part of the therapist.

Unfortunately the Alzheimer's patient cannot "rage" as Dylan Thomas would have him do. Too many mechanisms have been shut down for that rebellion to be possible. When a young and doubting art therapist asks me what contribution art therapy can make with such an impaired population facing certain deterioration, I come back with a story and a question. A man is dying, I say, and you have been requested to spend the last hour of his life with him. It is within your power to make that a rich, intimate, and fulfilling hour for him. You do so, the man smiles contentedly, and then he dies. There was no hope of improvement. Nothing has changed for him except for that gift that you gave him. Would you feel that your investment was validated? Was it a worthwhile endeavor? If you think that it wasn't, you might want to rethink your profession. Because this gift is what you have to give the Alzheimer's patient. This has to be enough. This act of the last hour has to be the inspiration of the therapist as he "rage[s] against the dying of the light," confirming his belief and respect for life. Herein lies the satisfaction and provision of the fuel to continue for all who take care of Alzheimer's patients in the last "hours" of their lives.

REFERENCES

Achterberg, J. (1985). *Imagery in healing.* Boston: Shambala.

Anzieu, D. (1989). *The skin ego.* New Haven, CT: Yale University Press.

Arieti, S. (1976). *Creativity: The magic synthesis.* New York: Basic Books.

Ariyoshi, S. (1972). *The twilight years.* Tokyo: Kodansha International.

Avni, S. (1998). *Photographs.* Ramat Gan: The Museum of Israeli Arts.

Bayley, J. (1999). *Elegy for Iris.* New York: St. Martin's Press.

Berardi, L. (1997). Art therapy with Alzheimer's patients: Struggling in a new reality. *Pratt Institute/Creative Arts Therapy Review, 18,* 23–32.

Byers, A. (1995). Beyond marks: On working with elderly people with severe memory loss. *Inscape, 1,* 13–18.

Cane, F. (1983). *The artist in each of us.* Washington, DC: Art Therapy Publications.

Cassou, M. (2001). *Point zero: Creativity without limits.* New York: Tarcher/Putnam.

Cerf, B., & Cartmell, U. H. (Eds.). (1994). *The best short stories of O. Henry.* New York: Random House.

Chetwynd, T. (1982). *Dictionary of symbols.* London: Aquarian/Thorsons.

Cirlot, J. E. (1971). *A dictionary of symbols.* New York: Barnes and Noble Books.

Clancier, A., & Kalmanovitch, J. (1987). *Winnicott and paradox from birth to creation.* London: Tavistock Publications.

Cohen, E. (2003). *The house on Beartown Road.* New York: Random House.

Cohen-Shalev, A. (1989). Old age style: Developmental changes in creative production from a life-span perspective. *Journal of Aging Studies, 3,* 21–37.

Cooney, E. (2003). *Death in slow motion: My mother's descent into Alzheimer's.* New York: HarperCollins.

Couch, J. B. (1997). Behind the veil: Mandala drawings by dementia patients. *Art Therapy: Journal of the American Art Association, 14,* 187–193.

Crosson, C. (1976). Art therapy with geriatric patients: Problems of spontaneity. *American Journal of Art Therapy, 15,* 51–57.

Crutch, S. J., Isaacs, R., & Rossor, M. N. (2001). Some workmen can blame their tools: Artistic change in an individual with Alzheimer's disease. *The Lancet, 357,* 2129–2133.

Cutting, L. K. (1997). *Memory slips: A memoir of music and healing.* New York: Harper Perennial.

Dalley, T. (Ed.) (1984). *Art as therapy: An introduction to the use of art as a therapeutic technique.* London: Tauestock.

Dalley, T., Case, C., Schaverien, J., Weir, F., Halliday, D., Hall, P. N., & Waller, D. (Eds.). (1987). *Images of art therapy: New developments in theory and practice.* London: Tavistock Publications/Routledge.

Davis, M., & Wallbridge, D. (1981). *Boundary and space: An introduction to the work of D. W. Winnicott.* New York: Brunner/Mazel Publishers.

Di Leo, J. H. (1973). *Children's drawings as diagnostic aids.* New York: Brunner/Mazel.

Dolginko, B. G., & Robbins, A. (2000). The institution as a holding environment for the therapist. In A. Robbins (Ed.), *The artist as therapist.* London: Jessica Kingsley.

Doric-Henry, L. (1997). Pottery as art therapy with elderly nursing home residents. *Art Therapy Journal of the American Art Therapy Association, 14,* 167–171.

Edwards, D. (1989). Five years on: Further thoughts on the issue of surviving as an art therapist. In A. Gilroy and T. Dalley (Eds.), *Pictures at an exhibition.* New York: Tavistock Publications/Routledge.

Ehrenzweig, A. (1971). *The hidden order of art: A study of the psychology of artistic imagination.* Berkeley: University of California Press.

Feil, N. (1993). *The validation breakthrough: Simple techniques for communicating with people with Alzheimer's-type dementia.* Baltimore: Health Professions Press.

Finnema, E., Droes, R. M., Ribbe, M., & Tilburg, W. van. (2000). A Review of psychosocial models in psychogeriatrics: Implications for care and research. *Alzheimer's Disease and Associated Disorders, 14,* 68–80.

Fromm, E. (1951). *The forgotten language.* New York: Grove Press.

Gone, J., Ring, H., Stern, M., & Soroker, N. (1992). Art therapy with stroke patients. *NeuroRehabilitation, 2,* 36–44.

Grant, L. (1999). *Remind me who I am, again.* London: Granta Books.

Growdon, J. H. (1985). Clinical profiles of Alzheimer's disease. In C. G. Gottfries (Ed.), *Normal aging, Alzheimer's disease, and senile dementia.* Edition de L'Universite de Bruxelles.

Harlan, J. (1990). Beyond the patient to the person: Promoting aspects of autonomous functioning in individuals with mild to moderate dementia. *The American Journal of Art Therapy, 28,* 99–105.

Hillman, J. (1999). *The force of character and the lasting life.* New York: Ballantine Books.

Ignatieff, M. (1994). *Scar tissue*. New York: Farrar, Straus and Giroux.

Jarvinen, P. J., & Gold, S. R. (1979). *Imagery as an aid in reducing depression*. New York: Third American Conference on the Fantasy and Imaging Process.

Jennings, K. (2002). *Moral hazard*. New York: Fourth Estate.

Jennings, S. (1986). *Creative drama in groupwork*. Oxon: Winslow Press.

Jensen, S. M. (1997). Multiple pathways to self: A multisensory art experience. *Art Therapy: Journal of the American Art Therapy Association, 14*, 178–186.

Johnson, C., Puracchio Lahey, P., & Shore, A. (1992). An exploration of creative arts therapeutic group work on an Alzheimer's unit. *Arts in Psychotherapy, 19*, 269–277.

Jung, C. G. (1963). *Memories, dreams, reflections*. London: Collins & Routledge & Kegan Paul.

Jung, C. G. (1964). *Man and his symbols*. London: Aldus Books.

Jung, C. G. (1986). *Selected writings*. London: Fontana Press.

Kahn-Denis, K. B. (1997). Art therapy with geriatric dementia clients. *Art Therapy: Journal of the American Art Therapy Association, 14*, 194–199.

Kamar, O. (1997). Light and death: Art therapy with a patient with Alzheimer's disease. *American Journal of Art Therapy, 35*, 118–124.

Kaufmann, W. (1970). *I and thou: Martin Buber*. New York: Touchstone.

Keyes, M. F. (1983). *Inward journey: Art as therapy*. La Salla, IL: Open Court.

Kitwood, T. (1997). *Dementia reconsidered: The person comes first*. Buckingham, UK: Open University Press.

Klein, I. (1987). *When the brain betrays the body* (Hebrew). Tel Aviv: Sifriat HaPoalim.

Knight, B. G. (1992). *Older adults in psychotherapy: Case histories*. London: Sage Publications.

Kohut, H. (1977). *The restoration of the self*. New York: International Universities Press.

Kramer, E. (1971). *Art as therapy with children*. New York: Schocken Books.

Landgarten, H. B. (1981). *Clinical art therapy*. New York: Brunner/Mazel.

Leibman, M. (1986). *Art therapy for groups*. Cambridge: Brookline Books.

Mangum, T. (1999). Teaching the patient impatience: Art, ageing, and the medical consumer. *The Lancet, 354*, Supplement 3.

Marcus, C. C. (1995). *House as a mirror of self*. Berkeley, CA: Conari Press.

Martindale, B. (1989). Becoming dependent again: The fears of some elderly persons and their younger therapists. *Psychoanalytic Psychotherapy, 4*, 67–75.

May, R. (1975). *The courage to create*. New York: Bantam Books.

McGowin, D. F. (1993). *Living in the labyrinth*. New York: Delta.

Miller, B. L., & Clausen, M. M. (1998). Rare cases of dementia stimulate artistic juices, offering unexpected window into the artistic process. *Science Daily Magazine* (University of California, San Francisco), October 21, http://www.sciencedaily.com/releases/1998/10/981021080231.htm.

Miller, S. (2003). *Story of my father*. New York: Knopf.

Mitchell, S. A. (1993). *Hope and dread in psychoanalysis*. New York: Basic Books.

Nadeau, R. (1984). Using the visual arts to expand personal creativity. In B. War-ren (Ed.), *Using the creative arts in therapy*. Cambridge, MA: Brookline Books.

Nash, J. M. (2000). The new science of Alzheimer's. *Time Europe, 156,* Number 3.

Naumberg, M. (1958). Art therapy: Its scope and function. In E. F. Hammer (Ed.), *Clinical applications of projective drawings*. Springfield: C. C. Thomas.

Parry, G., & Gowler, D. (1983). Career stresses of psychological therapists. In D. Pilgrim (Ed.), *Psychology and psychotherapy*. London: Routledge & Kegan Paul.

Plagens, P. (1997) The last Dutch master. *Newsweek,* March 31, pp. 53–54.

Read, H. A. (1959). *Concise history of modern painting*. London: Thames and Hudson.

Robbins, A., & Goffia-Girasek, M. S. (1987). Materials as an extension of the hold-ing environment. In A. Robbins (Ed.), *The artist as therapist*. New York: Human Sciences Press.

Robbins, A. (Ed.). (1987). *The artist as therapist*. New York: Human Sciences Press.

Rubin, J. A. (1984). *The art of art therapy*. New York: Brunner/Mazel.

Rubin, J. A. (1987). *Approaches to art therapy*. New York: Brunner/Mazel.

Russell, J. (1971). *Francis Bacon*. New York: Thames and Hudson.

Sacks, O. (1985). *The man who mistook his wife for a hat*. London: Picador.

Samuels, M., & Samuels, N. (1975). *Seeing with the mind's eye: The history, tech-niques, and uses of visualization*. New York: Random House.

Sartre, J. P. (1964). *Nausea*. New York: New Directions.

Schachtel, E. (1959). *Metamorphosis*. New York: Basic Books.

Schaverien, J. (1989). The picture within the frame. In A. Gilroy and T. Dalley (Eds.), *Pictures at an exhibition*. New York: Tavistock Publications/Routledge.

Schaverien, J. (1992). *The revealing image: Analytical art psychotherapy in theory and practice*. New York: Tavistock Publications/Routledge.

Schroder, K. A. (1999). *Egon Schiele. Eros & passion*. Munich: Prestel Verlag.

Sheikh, A. J., Mason, D., & Taylor, A. (1993). An experience of an expressive group with the elderly. *British Journal of Psychotherapy, 10,* 77–82.

Shenk, D. (2001). *The forgetting: Alzheimer's: Portrait of an epidemic*. New York: Doubleday.

Shore, A. (1997). Promoting wisdom: The role of art therapy in geriatric settings. *Art Therapy: Journal of the American Art Therapy Association, 14,* 172–177.

Siegelman, E. Y. (1990). *Metaphor and meaning in psychotherapy*. New York: The Guilford Press.

Silberman, S. (April, 2002). The fully immersive mind of Oliver Sacks. *Wired Magazine*.

Stolorow, R. D., Atwood, G. E., & Brandchaft, B. (Eds.). (1994). *The intersubjective perspective*. London: Jason Aranson.

Stronach-Buschel, B. (1991). Where the wild things are: A psychoanalytic art therapy perspective. *The Arts in Psychotherapy, 18,* 65–68.

Thomson, M. (1989). *On art and therapy.* London: Virago Press.

Tinnin, L. (1990). Biological processes in nonverbal communication and their role in the making and interpretation of art. *The American Journal of Art Therapy, 29,* 9–13.

Wadeson, H. (1980). *Art psychotherapy.* New York: John Wiley.

Wadeson, H., Durkin, J., & Perach, D. (Eds.). (1989). *Advances in art therapy.* New York: John Wiley and Sons.

Wald, J. (1983). Alzheimer's disease and the role of art therapy in its treatment. *American Journal of Art Therapy, 22,* 57–65.

Wald, J. (1986). Fusion of symbols, confusion of boundaries: Percept contamination in the art work of Alzheimer's disease patients. *Art Therapy, 3,* 74–80.

Wald, J. (1989). Art therapy for patients with Alzheimer's disease and related disorders. In H. Wadeson, J. Durent, D. Perach (Eds.), *Advances in Art therapy.* New York: John Wiley.

Waller, D. (1987). Art therapy in adolescence: A metaphorical view of a profession in progress. In T. Dalley, C. Case, J. Schaverien, F. Weir, D. Halliday, P. N. Hall, and D. Waller (Eds.), *Images of art therapy.* New York: Tavistock Publications/ Routledge.

Wallis, V. (1993). *Two old women: An Alaska legend of betrayal, courage, and survival.* Fairbanks, AK: Epicenter Press.

Warren, B. (1984). *Using the creative arts in therapy.* Cambridge: Brookline Books.

Weiss, J. C. (1984). *Expressive therapy with elders and the disabled.* New York: The Haworth Press.

Welty, E. (1995). *One writer's beginnings.* Boston: Harvard University Press.

Winnicott, D. W. (1971). *Playing and reality.* London: Tavistock Publications.

Winnicott, D. W. (1975). *Through pediatrics to psychoanalysis.* London: The Hogarth Press and the Institute of Psycho-Analysis.

Wolf, E. S. (1988). *Treating the self: Elements of clinical self psychology.* New York: Guilford Press.

Yalom, I. D. (1980). *Existential psychotherapy.* New York: Basic Books.

Zgola, J. (1987). *Doing things: A guide to programming activities for persons with Alzheimer's disease and related disorders.* Baltimore: Johns Hopkins University Press.

INDEX

About the Author

RUTH ABRAHAM is Senior Lecturer in Art Therapy for the Post Graduate Program at the Beit Berl College School of Art in Cfar Saba, Israel. She has worked for many years with Alzheimer's patients at a psychogeriatric center, and has also maintained a private clinic as an art therapist with the general population.